Child Health and Surveillance

Judith Moreton
Health Visitor
Oxfordshire Health Authority

Aidan Macfarlane
Consultant Community Physician
Oxfordshire Health Authority

SECOND EDITION

OXFORD

Blackwell Scientific Publications

LONDON EDINBURGH BOSTON

MELBOURNE PARIS BERLIN VIENNA

© 1980, 1991 by
Blackwell Scientific Publications
Editorial Offices:
Osney Mead, Oxford OX2 0EL
25 John Street, London WC1N 2BL
23 Ainslie Place, Edinburgh EH3
6AJ
3 Cambridge Center, Cambridge,
Massachusetts 02142, USA
54 University Street, Carlton
Victoria 3053, Australia

Other Editorial Offices:
Arnette SA
2, rue Casimir-Delavigne
75006 Paris
France

Blackwell Wissenschaft
Meinekestrasse 4
D-1000 Berlin 15
Germany

Blackwell MZV
Feldgasse 13
A-1238 Wien
Austria

First published 1980
Reprinted with corrections 1982
Reprinted 1984, 1986, 1988
Second edition 1991

Set by Setrite Typesetters,
Hong Kong
Printed and bound in Great Britain
at The Alden Press, Oxford

DISTRIBUTORS

Marston Book Services Ltd
  PO Box 87
  Oxford OX2 0DT
  (*Orders*: Tel: 0865 791155
             Fax: 0865 791927
             Telex: 837515)

USA
  Mosby-Year Book, Inc.
  11830 Westline Industrial Drive
  St. Louis, Missouri 63146
  (*Orders*: Tel: 800 633−6699)

Canada
  Mosby-Year Book, Inc.
  5240 Finch Avenue East
  Scarborough, Ontario
  (*Orders*: Tel: (416) 298−1588)

Australia
  Blackwell Scientific Publications
  (Australia) Pty Ltd
  54 University Street
  Carlton, Victoria 3053
  (*Orders*: Tel: (03) 347−0300)

British Library
Cataloguing in Publication Data

Moreton, Judith
  Child health and surveillance. —
  2nd ed.
  1. Children. Health
  I. Title II. Macfarlane, Aidan
  613.0432

  ISBN 0−632−01965−4

Contents

Acknowledgements

We are indebted to the following people who have helped us enormously by their contributions and suggestions: Liz Bixby, Paediatric Liaison Health Visitor; Carolyn Gordon, Speech Therapist; Kate Wortham, Senior Orthoptist; Chloe Fisher, Senior Nursing Officer, Midwifery; Mrs Barbara Hull, District Speech Therapist; Paula Hunt, Community Dietician; Sandy Pitt, School Nurse; Roger Cullen, Oxfordshire Conciliation Service; Dr Susan Huson, Department of Genetics; Ros McLeod, Health Visitor; Theresa Mumby, Oxfordshire Welfare Rights; Emma Knights, Oxfordshire Welfare Rights; Andrew Lane, Oxfordshire Money Advice Project; Kate Saffin, Senior School Nurse; Jill Pomerance, ACT, Bristol; Hilary Edmondson, Barley Hill Chemist, Thame.

We would particularly like to thank Sue Sefi, Research and Resource Officer, for her help in 'making sentences stand on their own', and Jeremy Piercy for correcting the typographical errors.

We would also like to thank the various authors and publishers listed below for permission to reproduce the following material:

The table on the risk of Down's syndrome, from 'Ante-natal Diagnosis in Early Pregnancy', by J.B. Scrimingeaur, *British Journal of Hospital Medicine*, 1978.

The table on the birth frequencies of common abnormalities, from 'Genetic Counselling', by C.O. Carter, *British Journal of Hospital Medicine*, 1978.

The table on the risk of abnormalities in children whose parents are affected from 'The Genetic Approach to Childhood Disorders', by Judith G. Hall; the table on diagnosing infant defects from 'Malformation', by David W. Smith; and the table on allergy manifestations from 'Allergy Disorders' by C. Warren Bierman and William E. Pierson; all in *Introduction to Clinical Paediatrics*, edited by David W. Smith, Saunders, Washington, 1977.

The table showing the normal intakes of healthy children from *Paediatric Vade Mecum*, edited by Dr Ben Wood, Lloyd-Luke Ltd, 1977.

The chart of substances known to have caused poisoning in children, from *Health Trends 1980*, HMSO.

The table showing accidental deaths by cause, age and sex, from *OPCS Mortality Statistics*, 1985.

The table showing accidents by age and sex, from *OPCS Quarterly Monitors DH4 Series*.

The chart showing the proportion of infants being breastfed in the first 9 months, from *OPCS Survey*, 1975, 1980 & 1985.

The table on the sources of vitamin deficiency in childhood, modified from *Diseases in Infancy and Childhood*, by Ellis & Mitchell, Churchill Livingstone, Edinburgh, 1973.

Two tables on vomiting and diarrhoea, adapted from the *Handbook of Paediatrics*, edited by H.K. Silver, C.H. Kemp & H.B. Bruyn, Lange, 1977.

The girl's and boy's growth charts, from Castlemead publications.

The table showing pubertal development, from *Growth*, by A. Aynsley-Green, Blackwell Scientific Publications, Oxford.

The table on recommendations on the use of EPI antigens, and the statement on breastfeeding and HIV, from the *AIDS Series 3*, World Health Organization, 1989.

The table on typical patterns of child development and accidents by age, and child restraint systems, from the Child Accident Prevention Trust.

The figures showing the structure of a DSS office, and the Social Security System, from the Barton Information Centre, Oxford.

The table on encopresis, from Dr. Gillian Forrest, Child Psychiatrist, Park Hospital, Oxford.

1 Child health maintenance

1.1 Surveillance and screening

A surveillance programme is an important part of child health care. It offers parents partnership with health professionals in providing an overview of the physical, social and emotional health and development of their children, thus working towards the goal that every child should reach his or her optimum level of health, and be able to maintain that optimum. This programme should be available to all children, including those with special needs, children of travelling families, those who are homeless and children of armed service personnel.

Screening tests do not attempt to make a diagnosis, but separate out a group who may be at high risk of having the problem the screening is designed to detect.

Record keeping and parent held child health records

In recognizing that parents are primarily responsible for the health of their children, and that only 20% of health symptoms are referred to either a doctor or health visitor, there is increasing emphasis on ensuring accurate documentation of each child's health needs (Saffin & Macfarlane, 1988). This documentation requires concise, orderly and legible recording.

The parents should hold the main child health record, so that the record is available whenever and wherever a child is seen — at home, at the surgery, child health clinic or hospital outpatients. The parents should also be active in recording their own observations and controlling the confidentiality of the record.

If families move from one area to another, the record would be immediately available to the new health care professionals, and would facilitate the transition into the school medical service.

1.2 Routine physical examination

Between 4 and 7% of children who survive the period immediately after birth have a congenital defect of some sort, and about half of these defects are recognized before the child leaves hospital. Most of the defects that are not recognized before the child leaves hospital should be picked up during routine examination before the end of the first year of life.

The following clues will lead to detection of defects that are usually not noted until after the neonatal period:

Mental deficiency   lag in developmental performance; neurological and behavioural aberrations

Deafness   limited monotonous vocalization; behavioural problems

Cataract   lack of red ocular reflex

Blindness   not following objects with eyes; developmental performance lag

Strabismus   most commonly internal and alternating

Pyloric stenosis   two-to-six-week age onset of non-bile-stained vomiting, becoming projectile

Malrotation of colon   bile-stained vomiting; abdominal distension

Meckel's diverticulum   rarely symptomatic; gastrointestinal bleeding, intussusception

Umbilical hernia   usually benign, generally disappear spontaneously

Inguinal hernia   may incarcerate, merits early closure

Obstructive valves, etc. in kidney   urinary tract infection plus failure to thrive

Hydronephrosis   urinary traction infection and failure to thrive, plus mass in upper quadrant

Inward tibial torsion   mild degrees normal, serious degrees merit treatment

Malalignment of feet   metatarsus adductus is one of the most common

Malalignment at hip   feet and knees noted to be in aberrant alignment

Hemangiomas   strawberry hemangiomas may appear after birth and usually begin to recede by 9 to 18 months

Recommended screening procedures

Before, during and after any examination, the parents should be asked if they have any concerns or queries.

Examination schedule

Neonatal examination

• Review family history, pregnancy and birth and discussion of any parental concerns or queries
• Measure weight and head circumference; check fontanelles
• Check eyes; movements and red ocular reflex
• Check palate for cleft
• Check skin for rashes, haemangioma, pigmentation, etc.
• Check hips for dislocation
• Listen to heart
• Check back for any signs of spina bifida occulta
• Does the baby respond to sound? — if high risk category consider referral
• Check general tone
• Check limb movements
• Are the genitalia normal? check testicular descent in boys and vaginal opening in girls
• Any signs of hernias?
• Any signs of talipes?
• Check hands, feet and ears for accessory digits or skin tags
• Blood tests for phenylketonuria and hypothyroidism. Sickle cell anaemia, galactosaemia and cystic fibrosis are screened for in some health districts

Within 10 days

• Check for congenital dislocation of the hips again

6–8 weeks

• Check history and parental concerns or queries
• Physical examination, weight and head circumference
• Check for congenital dislocation of the hips again

- Does the baby respond to sound? — if high risk category consider referral. Give parents checklist of advice for detection of hearing loss (Hints for Parents)
- Inspect the eyes
- If status of testicular descent not known from birth information, or if testes not fully descended at birth, check again

7–9 months
- Parental concerns or queries regarding health and development
- Check weight if parents request or if indicated
- Check for congenital dislocation of the hips
- Check for testicular descent if not previously recorded
- Observe visual behaviour and look for squint
- Carry out distraction test for hearing

18–24 months
- Parental concerns or queries particularly regarding behaviour, vision and hearing
- Confirm that the child is walking with normal gait
- Confirm that the child is beginning to speak, and is understanding when spoken to
- Arrange detailed assessment if either hearing or vision are in doubt
- Remember the high incidence of iron-deficiency anaemia at this age

36–42 months
- Parental concerns or queries
- Ask about vision, squint, hearing, behaviour and development
- If any concerns, discuss with parents whether the child is likely to have 'special educational needs' and arrange further action as appropriate
- Measure height and plot on centile chart
- Check for testicular descent unless previously fully descended
- Perform or arrange a hearing test if indicated

48–66 months — school entry

- Parental and teacher concerns or queries
- Review pre-school records
- Physical examination if specifically indicated.
- Auscultation of the heart if not performed since 6–8 week check
- Measure height and plot on centile chart
- Check vision using Snellen chart
- Check hearing by 'sweep' pure tone audiometry test

It is important that any child referred for specialist opinion at any stage of his/her development should be followed up to check the outcome of that referral.

1.3   Growth

The use of centile charts (Figs 1.1 and 1.2.)

Percentile charts are based on two kinds of data collected from normal children: cross sectional data — measuring and weighing large groups of children from different age groups at one time; or longitudinal data — following a number of children as they grow with regular weighings and measuring. In some charts both types of information are combined.

The percentile lines show the chances of a normal child falling above or below that line — for example the chances of a normal child falling above the 97th percentile is 3 in 100 and the chance of a child falling below the 3rd percentile is 3 in 100.

Children whose weight or height is below the third percentile deserve additional attention and possible evaluation by a paediatrician. Similarly those whose head circumference is above the 97th or below the 3rd percentile may also need evaluation.

1.4   Weight

Weight is the most widely used clinical measurement of growth, although it cannot be regarded as a screening procedure. Most importantly it reassures the parents that their baby is thriving.

Weight gain is widely used as a clinical measurement of growth and can be a useful index of illness, poor nutrition and emotional deprivation. Most babies who gain weight slowly, or whose weight gradually crosses centile lines downwards are in fact normal. Rapid downwards crossing of the centiles, weight loss, or prolonged failure to gain weight suggest the presence of pathology.

Common causes of poor weight gain
- Underfeeding
- Environmental and sociopsychological deprivation
- Malabsorptions, e.g. coeliac disease, cystic fibrosis
- Other chronic diseases and chronic infections
- Recognizable congenital syndromes
- Congenital heart disease
- Neuroendocrinal or metabolic diseases

Recommendations for weighing
Weighing should be available at each clinic visit, or at the parents' request. However, too frequent weighing can produce unnecessary anxiety or worry for parents.

Methods of weighing
- Babies should be weighed nude, unless there are splints or dressings
- Scales should be checked and calibrated regularly
- Measurements should be dated and plotted on centile charts
- Correction for gestational age should be made — so that a baby born at 33 weeks gestation, for instance, will have the birth weight recorded on the 33 week line and subsequent weights are plotted from that line

It must be remembered that there may be considerable variation in weight owing to such factors as different scales, whether the child has a full/empty bladder, and how recently the baby was fed.

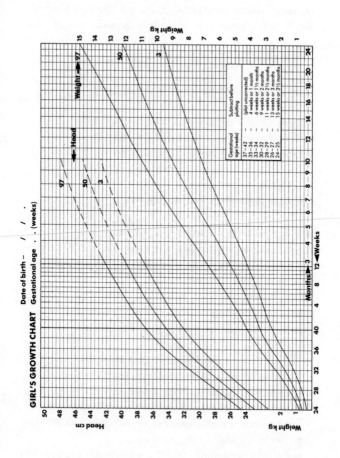

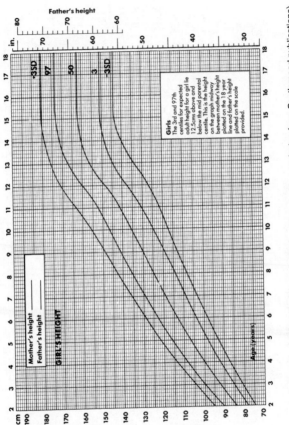

Girls

The 3rd and 97th centiles for expected adult height for a girl lie 12.5cms above and below the mid parental centile. This is the height on the graph midway between mother's height plotted on the 18 year line and father's height plotted on the scale provided.

Fig. 1.1 Girl's growth assessment chart (reproduced with permission from Castlemead publications).

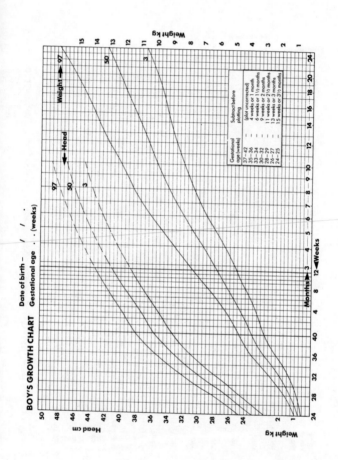

BOY'S GROWTH CHART

Date of birth – / / .

Gestational age . . (weeks)

Head cm

Weight kg

Gestational age (weeks)	Subtract before plotting
37 – 42	(plot uncorrected)
35 – 36	4 weeks or 1 month
33 – 34	6 weeks or 1½ months
30 – 32	9 weeks or 2 months
28 – 29	11 weeks or 2½ months
26 – 27	13 weeks or 3 months
24 – 25	15 weeks or 3½ months

Weight → 97

Head ←

Weight kg

Months ◄

Weeks

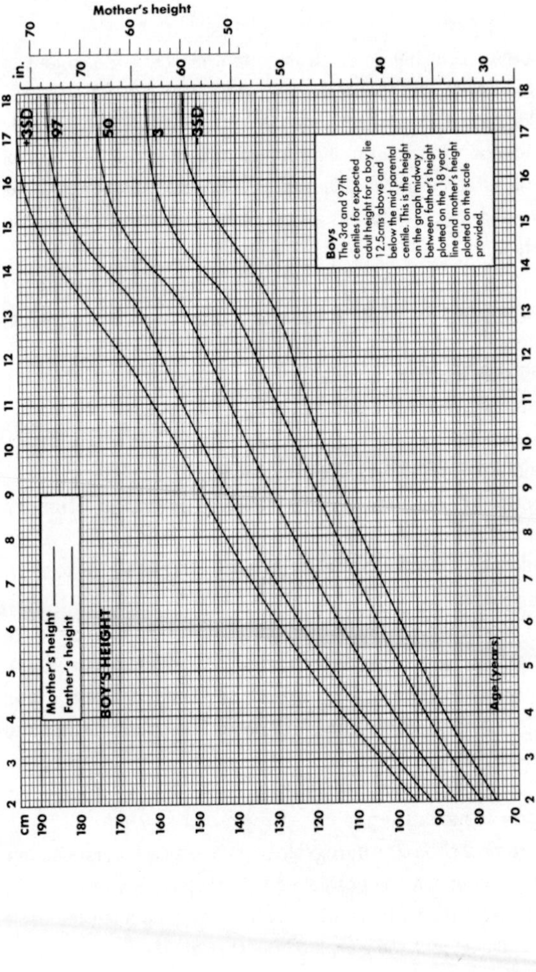
Mother's height
in.
cm
+3SD
97
50
3
-3SD
Mother's height
Father's height
BOY'S HEIGHT
Age (years)
Boys
The 3rd and 97th centiles for expected adult height for a boy lie 12.5cms above and below the mid parental centile. This is the height on the graph midway between father's height plotted on the 18 year line and mother's height plotted on the scale provided.

Fig. 1.2 Boy's growth assessment chart (reproduced with permission from Castlemead publications).

Referral
- Any child who causes concern, either to the parents or health professionals
- Children who consistently cross the centile lines downwards

1.5 Height

Measurement of height is an important clinical assessment of skeletal growth and should be performed from 2 years onwards. Results should always be plotted on a percentile chart. There is no evidence to support routine measurement in the first year of life, unless some growth disorder is suspected. Excessively tall stature should be detected as psychological problems may be important.

Aetiologies of short stature
- Familial
- Low birth weight
- Slow maturation
- Poor environmental circumstances
- Organic diseases, e.g. coeliac disease, cystic fibrosis
- Congenital syndromes, e.g. Down's syndrome, Turner's syndrome
- Endocrine disorders, e.g. growth hormone deficiency, hypothyroidism

An Oxfordshire study showed that of 227 children referred for short stature, 60% were 'short normal', 9% had hypothyroidism, 7% Turner's syndrome, 6% growth hormone deficiency, and 18% manifested other causes (Aynsley Green & Macfarlane, 1983).

Methods of measuring

Measurement should be by microtoise, with a magnetic measuring device or an accurately positioned wall measuring chart.
- The child must be measured with bare feet together, the back of the heels against the wall, the bottom of the heels on the floor, and the feet together

- The head must face forward
- The chin should be tilted so that the eye is level with the ear
- If using a chart, the centre of the head should be against the appropriate age line
- Measure the height from the top of the head

Recommendations
- Children should be measured routinely between 2 and 3 years of age and again at 4½ to 5 years
- Measurements beyond age 5 should be made if:
  (a) there is doubt about the significance of previous measurements, or
  (b) if previous records are incomplete or unsatisfactory.

Action
- If the measurement is below the 3rd centile but above the −3 SD line, then action must be taken to decide if parental short stature is an adequate explanation
- If the measurement is below the −3 SD line specialist opinion should be considered
- If at the 4−5 year check, the height is below the 3rd centile or a significant shift across the centiles is suspected, then a further measurement should be taken not less than 6 months later
- Further opinion should be considered if there is doubt after two measurements
- If parents or health professionals are concerned

1.6 Head circumference

Routine head measurement is designed to detect those disorders characterized by a small head, and those by a large head. Since 3% of children have a head circumference above the 97th centile, and 3% have a head circumference below the 3rd centile, other evidence must be sought to determine whether a particular measurement is significant.

Aetiologies

Small heads may be caused by

- Small baby
- Familial tendency — some ethnic groups have small heads
- Mental subnormality (including congenital disorders)
- Craniostenosis
- Abnormal neurological development

Large heads may be caused by

- Large baby
- Familial feature
- Hydrocephalus
- Subdural effusion and haematoma
- Conditions associated with dysmorphic syndromes

Measurement of the head

This should be done with a paper or plastic tape at the maximum circumference around the supraorbital ridges and glabella and the maximal point of the occiput.

Recommendations for measurement

Before discharge from hospital and then at 6−8 weeks. Care should be taken that the method of measurement is correct and that correction is made for gestational age. Both measurements should be recorded in figures and plotted on the centile chart. If there is no concern at this time, no further measurements are necessary.

Referral

- Child shows symptoms or signs compatible with hydrocephaly or other abnormality
- Head circumference curve which deviates away from the 97th or the 3rd centile, or crosses centiles without the same evolution of the weight curve
- Parental or professional anxiety

1.7 Pubertal development

Puberty is the period during which sexual maturation takes place. Its onset is influenced by hereditary factors, race and nutrition. The normal timetable for pubertal development is shown in Tables 1.1–1.4.

Precocious puberty is usually defined as the onset of pubertal characteristics before the age of 8 in girls, and 10 in boys. This is 5 times more common in boys than girls, and in the majority of cases no cause can be found. However, any child with precocious puberty should nevertheless be referred to a paediatrician for further investigation.

Delayed puberty is defined as the absence of sexual development by the age of 13 in girls, and 15 in boys. The most common cause of delayed puberty is constitutional delay of growth in adolescence. All children who show delayed puberty should nevertheless be referred to a paediatrician for further investigation.

Table 1.1 Timetable for the development of puberty in the average boy

Age (years)	Pubertal characteristic
Before 10	Infantile state
11–12	Increase in testicular volume
12–13	Appearance of pubic hair (pubarche); penis begins to enlarge; increase in height velocity
13–14	Progressive enlargement of testes and penis; increase in pubic hair; appearance of first sesamoid bone of thumb
14	Peak height velocity
14–15	Appearance of moustache; pubic hair of adult type but not spread on to medial surface of thighs; axillary hair appears
15–16	Breaking of voice; pubic hair of full adult type; full growth of penis and testes with mature spermatozoa
17–19	Increase in facial and body hair; pubic hair of full adult type; fusion of the epiphyses and growth arrest

Table 1.2 Timetable for the development of puberty in the average girl

Age (years)	Pubertal characteristic
Before 8	Infantile state
10–11	Appearance of breast buds (thelarche); acceleration in growth; maturation of the vaginal mucosa
11	Appearance of pubic hair (pubarche) and sesamoid bone of thumb
12–13	Progressive growth of internal and external genitalia; pubic hair spread sparsely over junction of pubes, coarse and slightly curled; peak height velocity
13	Menarche occurs; appearance of axillary hair; pubic hair of adult type but not spread onto medial surface of thighs; projection of areola and papilla to form secondary mound above level of breast.
14–15	Regular ovulatory menstrual cycles, pregnancy possible; pubic hair of adult type and breast development at fully mature stage
15–16	Fusion of the epiphyses and arrest of growth

Table 1.3 Tanner sexual maturity stages in girls

Stage	Pubic hair	Breasts
1	Preadolescent	Preadolescent
2	Sparse, slightly pigmented, straight, medial border of labia	Breasts and papillae elevated as small mounds, areolar diameter increased
3	Hair darker, beginning to curl, increased amount	Breasts and areolas enlarged, no contour separation
4	Coarse, curly, abundant, but amount less than an adult	Areolas and papillae form secondary mound
5	Adult, feminine triangle spread to medial surface of thighs	Mature, nipples project, areolae part of general breast contour

1.8 Vision

Nine per cent of all children by the age of 6 will have attended an eye clinic either for active treatment or surveillance of an eye condition. Early detection is important as some serious conditions,

Table 1.4 Tanner sexual maturity stages in boys

Stage	Pubic hair	Penis
1	None	Preadolescent
2	Scanty, long, slightly pigmented	Slight enlargement
3	Darker, starts to curl, small amount	Longer
4	Resembles adult type but less in quantity, coarse and curly	Larger, glans increased in size and breadth
5	Adult distribution, spread to medial surface of thighs	Adult size

In boys, the process from pubic hair 2 to pubic hair 5 is about two years; and in girls, about two and one-half years. From breast stage 2 to menarche is about two and one-half years.

for example glaucoma, buphthalmos (cataract) and retino-blastoma, are surgically treatable. Squints and amblyopia are more effectively treated in the early stages, and other conditions have genetic implications or may be the presenting feature of serious systemic disease.

Babies can see from birth with a limited focus of 20 cm. Normal adult vision is present from about 4 to 6 months of age. Developmental guidance for parents with partially sighted or blind children can reduce secondary disabilities such as behaviour problems.

Aetiologies and risk factors
Causes of severe visual handicap in children
- Congenital conditions (inherited, multiple malformative syndromes or prenatal infections)
- Optic atrophy
- Retrolental fibroplasia
- Retinoblastoma
- Others such as postnatal eye or brain infection or trauma, perinatal insults

Risk factors
- Family history of
  (a) squints
  (b) ocular disorders before 6 years
  (c) wearing glasses before 10 years
  (d) retinoblastoma, glaucoma
- Prenatal infection
- Perinatal insults
- Genetic syndromes and other malformations
- Postnatal infection (eye or brain)
- Trauma (head or eye)
- Oxygen therapy in the neonatal period — retinopathy of prematurity
- Child abuse (head shaking)

Any child at risk of genetic visual disorders, major neurological defects (e.g. cerebral palsy), neurological conditions, or at risk of retinopathy of prematurity should undergo specialist eye examination.

Screening

Screening in the pre-school years should be confined to history, ocular appearance and active questioning. A test for visual acuity should be carried out at school entry (see pp. 20 and 162).

History
- Check risk factors — see above
- Do the parents think the baby/child can see normally?
- Are they worried about the baby/child's eyes?

Ocular appearance
- Do the baby/child's eyes look normal? Is the gaze steady?

Parental concern
It is important to ask about and listen to the parents' description of their baby/child's visual behaviour. A proportion, however, will not have noticed or believe that anything is wrong.

Active questioning of parents

Does their baby

- look at them?
- follow moving objects with the eyes?
- fixate small objects?

Common vision defects

Refractive error

Disturbance of the optical system prevents a sharp image from being formed precisely on the retina. Most people have some refractive errors which change throughout life. Many children will become short-sighted in their teens but will not have presented with problems before.

Amblyopia

The brain either suppresses or fails to develop the ability to differentiate detailed images from the affected eye. This may result from refractive errors, differences in refraction between the eyes, squints, or other conditions which prevent the image reaching the retina; for example ptosis or cataracts.

Squints

Manifest squints are present under normal seeing conditions, but may be intermittently controlled. A manifest squint is often first recognized by parents or relatives, and parents should be asked if they have ever noticed any squint, laziness or turning of one eye.

Cover/uncover test for strabismus

This can be carried out from 4 months of age. Visual fixation is obtained by showing the child an interesting object, such as a toy which collapses when the bottom is pressed. For children over 2 years, the object must contain detail to encourage the child to focus fully. When the child is fixating the object, each eye is covered in turn.

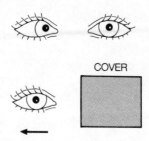

Fig. 1.3 Cover/uncover test for squint.

Note that in Figure 1.3 the right eye moves out to take up fixation. A squint may be inward turning, outward turning, up or downward turning. The important thing to remember is that the *uncovered* eye has to move to look directly at the object when a squint is present.

Special note should be made if the child objects strongly to one eye being covered as there may be defective vision of the other eye. However, many children around 18 months of age dislike either eye being covered!

Visual acuity

This is the measure of how well an individual can discriminate detail. Measurement under 3 years is very difficult as it requires the child's co-operation. Tests such as Sheridan's graded balls and matching toy test merely demonstrate the developmental stage at which visual fixation and concentration on tiny objects is reached. Other more specialized tests are being developed but are of limited availability.

Visual acuity test

From 9 months of age a child's visual awareness and location of objects should be watched. A 'serious' child who does not smile in response may be a child with visual difficulties.

At school entry a Snellen test should be performed in a well-lit, quiet room at 6 metres distance. Each eye should be tested separately. The Sheridan–Gardiner single letter test may be used if the child cannot manage the Snellen chart.

Ability to do the test is noticeably slower with the amblyopic eye, and vision recorded is usually at least one line less. Single letter vision is often much better than line vision because detail is difficult to discriminate when surrounded by other detail. Hence a 6/9 single letter vision may only be a 6/36 line vision.

Colour vision defects

Deficiencies in colour discrimination, primarily affecting red and green, occur in 8% of boys and about 0.5% of girls. A test should be offered to all 10 year olds, because colour defects prevent entry into certain careers and it may be helpful in future career planning.

1.9 Hearing

Early diagnosis of a hearing defect is important as it may interfere with language development, learning, social and emotional well-being (Table 1.5).

Those responsible for testing children's hearing should also have their own hearing tested every 2 years. Proper facilities for hearing tests must be provided and all staff involved with screening tests for hearing should have access to a sound level meter. A whispered voice for testing hearing should not be a 'front of mouth' voice, but should have a laryngeal component pitched below 30 decibels.

Causes of deafness

1 Sensorineural hearing loss is caused by a lesion in the cochlea or auditory nerve and its central connections, and may be unilateral or bilateral. Causes include intrauterine infections, for example rubella or cytomegalovirus (CMV), severe neonatal jaundice, meningitis or a genetic condition.

2 Conductive hearing loss is usually caused by secretory otitis media (glue ear), a foreign body or rarely malformation of the ear.

Table 1.5 The detection of deafness in babies

	0–3 months	3–6 months	6–9 months	9–12 months	1 year
Responses of normal babies to different sounds					
Loud Repeated	Startle Startle	Startle Startle	Slight movement Nil	Localizes Nil	Localizes Nil
Soft *Familiar* Voice with laryngeal component	May stop breathing for a moment; may turn head to sound	Quietens Smiles Vocalizes Stretches Trembles	Vocalizes Localizes immediately	Vocalizes Copies	Vocalizes Copies
Rattle	Nil or may turn head to sound	May turn head or eyes	Localizes on level	Localizes up or down	Habituates, loses interest on repetition
Cup	Nil	Quietens, may turn eyes, sucks, licks lips	Localizes	Localizes	Localizes and habituates
Unfamiliar	Nil	Nil, may move	Looks up once	May localize once	Localizes

Responses of deaf babies to different sounds

Loud	Nil	Nil; but may startle if very loud	Startle	Startle
Soft				
Voice	Nil	Nil or startle	Nil or startle	Fails to copy
Rattle	Nil	Nil or startle	Nil or startle	Nil or startle
Cup	Nil	Nil, fails to localize	Nil	Vague responses

NB If deafness is suspected, enquire about possible disease, drugs, other defects, family disease, delivery difficulties, deprivation. Deaf and deprived babies *do* vocalize and cry, but with monotonous and meagre sounds after 6 months.
Deprived babies respond to the above familiar sounds as if unfamiliar, failing to copy voice or localize.

At birth babies can hear and respond best to a female voice. Babies should startle to a loud sound and turn their eyes and/or head. This is normal up to about 4 to 5 months. However, children rapidly habituate to the same sound repeated many times, and cease to turn to it (Table 1.5)

If the carer is concerned the child should always be referred

Testing schedule
Neonatal screening such as the auditory response cradle, is still at the research stage and areas with such facilities generally use them for selective screening of high risk groups.

0−7 months
- Do the parents think the child can hear normally?
- Does the baby (up to 4 months) startle to loud sounds?
- Does the baby turn head and/or eyes to the mother's voice?

7−12 months
- Do the parents think the child can hear normally?
- Distraction test. This requires two people working together. The child is tested at 3 feet from each ear while sitting on the mother's knee with some form of visual stimulation in the midline to attract the child's attention initially. Always keep the sound source behind the level of the mother's chair.

Presenting sounds
Each sound must be presented to each ear.
- Voice 'oo'
- Voice 'ss'
- High tone rattle
- Low minimal voice, e.g. 'how are you baby?'

To pass the baby must turn his or her head. Failures should be retested in 2−4 weeks. If they fail again they should be referred.

18 months−5 years

Screening between these ages is no longer recommended. Audiological assessment should always be arranged for any child with

- Significantly impaired language development
- A history of chronic or repeated middle ear disease or upper airway obstruction
- Developmental or behavioural problems
- A history of meningitis or prolonged treatment with ototoxic drugs
- Any child where the parents are concerned

All hearing impaired children and their parents should have access to a centre with comprehensive audiological, diagnostic and treatment facilities, as well as genetic, paediatric and psychological advice.

School entry

- Do the parents think the child can hear normally?
- Check hearing with the 'sweep' test consisting of a modified pure tone audiogram performed at fixed intensity

1.10 Congenital dislocation of the hip

Congenital dislocation of the hip (CDH) is a potentially crippling disorder, with a high degree of handicap and orthopaedic problems in childhood and adulthood if not recognized early. It is impossible to detect every case at birth, and there must be continuing surveillance, until the child is seen to be walking normally.

The incidence of unstable hips in the neonate is 1.5−2%, but of these only 10% become dislocated and a further 10% may show signs of subluxation or dysplasia.

Risk factors

- Genetic
  (a) family history
  (b) female

- Gestational
  - (a) breech presentation
  - (b) uterine malformations
  - (c) oligohydramnios
  - (d) caesarean section
  - (e) first baby
  - (f) fetal growth retardation
- Other congenital malformations, especially of the feet

Screening

- Within 24 hours of birth
- At the time of discharge or within 10 days
- At 6−8 weeks of age
- At 6−9 months
- 15−21 months − when the child is walking

The gait should be reviewed at 24−30 months and again at preschool or school entry examination.

Screening tests

Ortolani/Barlow's manoeuvre. This method of examination is suitable for infants up to 3 months of age.

1 The examiner's hands should be warm, the examination gentle and the baby relaxed and undressed from the waist down.

2 The infant lies on his/her back with legs towards the examiner, and the hips adducted and fully flexed.

3 For examination of the left hip the examiner steadies the infant's pelvis with the thumb of the left hand on the symphysis pubis and the fingers under the sacrum.

4 The upper thigh of the left leg is held in the examiner's right hand with the middle finger over the greater trochanter, with the flexed leg held in the palm, and with the thumb on the inside of the thigh opposite the lesser trochanter.

5 The hip and leg are turned inward (adducted), attempting to move the femoral head gently forwards into and backwards out of the acetabulum.

6 In the first part of the manoeuvre, the middle digit is pressed upon the greater trochanter in an attempt to relocate the posteriorly placed head of the femur forwards into the acetabulum. If the head is felt to move (usually not more than 0.5 cm) with or without a palpable and/or audible 'clunk', then the dislocation is present.

7 The second part tests for instability. With the thumb on the inner side of the thigh, backward pressure is applied to the head of the femur. If the head is felt to move backwards over the labrum (the fibrocartilaginous rim of the acetabulum) on to the posterior aspect of the joint capsule (again a movement of not more than 0.5 cm, and often accompanied by a 'clunk'), then the hip is said to be subluxatable or unstable.

To examine the right hip, the role of the examiner's hands is reversed.

Abduction test. Limitation of abduction is the most important sign of dislocation and this test should be carried out at all ages. The infant lies on his/her back with the hips flexed to 90°.

1 Both hips can be abducted at the same time, with limitation noted in one hip or the other, or both in bilateral dislocation. Thighs normally abduct to 75° or:

2 One hip at a time may be abducted with the pelvis stabilized with the other hand to prevent tipping.

Classic signs of dislocation

Unilateral dislocation
- Leg posture: the affected side tends to be held in partial lateral rotation, flexion and abduction
- Limb shortening: above knee shortening on the affected side; when the hips are flexed, compare knee levels
- Asymmetry: skin creases may be asymmetrical when checked in supine and prone positions (not very reliable)
- Flattening of the buttock: may appear on the affected side in prone position

- Limitation of abduction: the most important sign — persistent and less than 75°

Bilateral dislocation
The signs are as described although there is no normal hip for comparison. A perineal gap may be apparent.

Gait
20% of children with CDH will not be walking at 18 months; however, the remaining 80% will stand and walk at normal age. A child with unilateral dislocation will limp or fall towards the affected side. After 2 years the child cannot balance on the affected leg. In bilateral dislocation the gait is waddling.

Referral
- All children with abnormal Ortolani/Barlow manoeuvre
- All children with one or more classic signs
- All children with gait problems
- All children where there is parental concern
- Any child where there are doubts or who has risk factors

1.11 Cryptorchidism (undescended testes)

Cryptorchidism is a condition where one or both testes fail to descend to a normal position in the scrotum. The condition is bilateral in about 10% of cases and in the majority of boys occurs without any association with other malformations.

The incidence and prevalence varies according to gestational age and the age of the child (Table 1.6). A high proportion descend normally by 3 months of age, but further natural descent is unlikely after this age.

Aetiology and risk factors
The aetiology of cryptorchidism is unclear, although hormonal causes seem to be implicated.
- Low birth weight — less then 2500 g
- Prematurity

Table 1.6 The prevalence of cryptorchidism

Age of child	Prevalence (%)
At birth	7.1*
2–3 months	1.6*
12 months	1.3

An additional 1.3% develop UDT.

* The prevalence is considerably higher for low-birthweight babies.

Figures taken from the first 12 months of the Oxford Cryptorchidism Study Group (John Radcliffe Hospital Cryptorchidism Study Group 1986a).

• Associated inguinal hernia
• Born to primigravidas
• Born to mothers under 20 years
• Breech delivery
• Mothers exposed to exogenous oestrogen therapy during first trimester

Early detection and referral

It is important to screen for undescended testes before 18 months of age for the following reasons:

1 Rising infertility rates. Low sperm counts occur in 100% of bilateral untreated cases and 75% of bilateral treated cases. The advantage of therapy to fertility in unilateral cases is unclear
2 There is an increased risk of malignancy
3 There is an increased risk of testicular torsion

Testing

1 The test is most easily performed at birth when there is a relatively large scrotum, minimal subcutaneous fat and the cremasteric reflex is absent.
2 Palpation requires a warm, relaxed baby who is lying down and a gentle examiner with warm hands. Each side of the scrotum should be examined separately.
3 If the testis cannot be felt in the scrotal sac, then the testis should be milked along the inguinal line from the internal to the

external ring, where it can be caught by the other hand and pulled gently into the scrotum as far as it will come.

Recommendations and referral
When the testes are fully descended, the parents should be told, and the fact recorded. All boys, including the handicapped, should be examined and treated.

1 Boys whose testes are both well down at birth do not need to be followed.

2 Boys whose testes are other than well down in the scrotum at birth — i.e. impalpable, very high in the inguinal pouch or scrotum, or that retract after being milked down — should be followed up until 5 years to identify retractile testes.

3 All boys whose testis/es are not descended by 1 year should be referred to a paediatric surgeon.

4 Refer any boy where the parents are anxious or wish a second opinion.

5 In case of doubt, refer.

1.12 Heart murmurs

Six to eight children per thousand are born with congenital heart disease (CHD), but innocent or physiological murmurs are present in more than 50% of all children and adolescents. It is important for doctors involved in surveillance to be able to distinguish between innocent murmurs and significant heart disease, and to identify other signs and symptoms of CHD.

Risk factors
• Family history of CHD or other malformations, i.e. renal
• Problems in pregnancy, e.g. infections, X-ray, alcohol, tobacco, drugs, systemic diseases, etc.
• Delivery — low or high birthweight, anoxia, resuscitation
• Neonatal problems, e.g. infection, respiratory distress
• Recognizable genetic syndromes or other malformations

Other signs and symptoms
- Feeding problems and/or failure to thrive
- Central cyanosis
- Clubbing
- Rapid respiratory rate
- Peripheral arterial pulses (radial/brachial and femoral)
- Blood pressure — using an appropriate paediatric cuff which covers two-thirds of the upper arm
- Shortness of breath on exertion
- Late walking
- Excessive tiredness
- Excessive sweating
- Squatting
- Recurrent lower respiratory tract infections
- Chest pains
- Palpitations or syncope
- Heart sounds — loudness and wide or fixed splitting of second sound or clicks
- Abnormal apex beat or precordium bulge

Examination
Children should be examined at birth, at 6−8 weeks and opportunistically up to 4½ to 5½ years, at which age examination should be carried out on school entry.
The murmur should be listened to
- Standing or sitting and supine
- In inspiration and expiration
- Over the left and right side of the front of the chest, the back and the neck
- A jugular venous hum will disappear when auscultated with the feet higher than the head
Innocent murmurs are
- Systolic with no diastolic component
- Soft, graded 3/6 or less
- Short ejection murmurs
- Well localized without radiation

Table 1.7 'Quick' developmental assessment

Age	Gross motor	Visual motor	Language	Social
1 month	Raises head slightly from prone, makes crawling movements	Has tight grip, follows to midline	Alerts to sound (by blinking, moving standing)	Regards face
2 months	Holds head in midline	No longer clenches fist tightly, follows object past midline	Smiles after being stroked or talked to	Increasingly alert
4 months	Sits well when propped	Grasps with both hands co-ordinated, touches cube placed on table	Orients to voice 5 months: turns head to bell, says 'ah-goo'	Enjoys looking
6 months	Rolls from back to front, sits well, puts feet in mouth in supine position	Reaches with either hand, transfers, uses raking grasp	Babbles 7 months: waves bye-bye 8 months: 'dada/mama' inappropriately	Recognizes strangers; plays pat-a-cake
9 months	Creeps, pulls to feet, likes to stand	Uses overhand pincer grasp, probes with forefinger, holds bottle, finger feeds	Imitates sounds 10 months: 'dada/mama' appropriately 11 months: 1 word	Starts to explore environment

12 months	Walks with hand held or alone, pivots when sitting, co-operates with dressing	Uses pincer grasp, throws objects, lets go of toys	Follows one-step command with gesture uses 2 words *14 months*: uses 3 words	Imitates actions, comes when called, co-operates with dressing
18 months	Runs, throws toys from standing without falling	Turns 2–3 pages at a time, fills spoon and feeds	Knows 7–20 words, points to named part of body, uses mature jargoning with intelligible words	Copies parents (e.g. in sweeping, dusting), plays with other children
2 years	Walks up and down steps without help	Turns pages one at a time, removes shoes, pants, etc.	Uses 50 words, 2-word phrases, pronouns, names objects in pictures	
3 years	Pedals tricycle, alternates feet when going up steps	Partial dressing and undressing, dries hands if reminded	Tells stories about experiences, knows his/her sex	Shares toys, takes turns, plays well with others
4 years	Hops, skips, alternates feet when going downstairs	Buttons clothes fully, catches ball	Knows all colours, recites song or poem from memory	Tells 'tall stories', plays co-operatively

These are approximate ages. Sometimes a child may skip a stage, such as crawling, and walk at 13 months, or 'bottom shuffle' instead of crawl and not walk until 18 months or later. Each child is an individual and parents sometimes need reassurance when they try to compare their child's development with others.

- Never accompanied by a thrill
- Louder on exercise, fever or anxiety
- Not accompanied by abnormal heart sounds
- Without any other signs and/or symptoms of cardiac disease

Pathological heart murmurs requiring referral

- All diastolic murmurs
- All pansystolic murmurs
- All late systolic murmurs
- Louder than 3/6 grade and accompanied by a thrill
- Continuous murmurs (except venous hum)
- Any murmur heard at the back
- Most murmurs transmitted to the neck — except venous hums
- Murmurs with other signs/symptoms of cardiac disease

Referral

1 All children where there is suspicion or doubt
2 Any child with signs and/or symptoms of heart disease
3 If the parents are anxious after discussion

It is important that innocent heart murmurs should be treated accordingly, and the parents assured that the child can lead a normal life and that antibiotic prophylaxis is not necessary.

1.13 Developmental assessment

Routine developmental testing of all pre-school or school children is unnecessary. However, parents' concerns should be taken seriously and referral to the appropriate professional expert for assessment should be readily available.

A quick developmental assessment is available in Table 1.7.

Further reading and references

Aynsley Green A., Macfarlane J.A. (1983) Method for the earlier recognition of abnormal stature, *Arch Dis Child* **58**, 535—7

Boothman R., Orr N. (1978) Screening for deafness in the first year of life, *Arch Dis Child* **53**, 570—3

Chalmers D. *et al*. (1989) *Otitis Media with Effusion in Children — The Dunedin Study*, MacKeith Press, London

Cochrane A., Holland W. (1969) Validation of screening procedures, *Br Med Bull* **27**, 3—8

DHSS (1986) *Screening for the Detection of Congenital Dislocated Hip*, HMSO, London

Goldson G. (1987) Failure to thrive: an old problem revisited. In *Progress in Child Health* (ed. Macfarlane J.A.) vol 13, Churchill Livingstone, Edinburgh

Hall D.M.B. (1989) *Health For All Children*, Oxford University Press, Oxford

John Radcliffe Hospital Cryptorchidism Study Group (1986a) Cryptorchidism: an apparent increase since 1960, *Br Med J* **293**, 1404−6

Kendall J.A. *et al.* (1989) Ocular Defects in Children from Birth to 6 years, *Br J Ophthalmol* **46**, 3−6

Macfarlane A., Sefi S., Cordeiro M. (1989) *Child Health − the Screening Tests*, Oxford University Press, Oxford

McCormick B. (1988) *Screening for Hearing Impairment in Young Children*, Croom Helm, London and Sydney

Polnay L., Hull D. (1985) *Community Paediatrics*, Churchill Livingstone, London

Saffin K., Macfarlane A. (1988) Parent held child health and development records, *Matern Child Nurs J* October 288−91

Scott D.J., Rigby M.L., Miller G.A.H., Shinebourne E.A. (1984) The presentation of symptomatic heart disease based on 10 years' experience (1973−82): implications for the provision of services, *Br Heart J* **52**, 248−57

Tanner J.M. (1978) *Foetus into Man*, Harvard University Press, Cambridge, Massachusetts

2   Health education

Health education is defined as 'any activity which promotes health related learning, i.e. some relatively permanent change in an individual's capabilities or dispositions' (Hall, 1989).

Health care professionals are in a prime position to offer continuing health education against a background of existing knowledge. By encouraging parents to accept responsibility for their own and their child's health, it is possible to change attitudes and behaviour.

Health promoting activities should include encouraging healthy eating and exercise, the prevention of tooth decay and accidents, immunization and prevention of iron deficiency anaemia.

2.1 Socioeconomic aspects of health care

The majority of children grow up in families, with the primary responsibility for child health being first and foremost a family concern. Specifically, the welfare of children is determined by the parents' capacity to provide safe accommodation, a good diet and access to health care as well as protecting them from physical and mental trauma. However, it is recognized that health promoting resources are not randomly distributed across the population, and children who benefit from a safe home are more likely to benefit from good food and health care as well.

The perinatal mortality (number of stillbirths and first week deaths per 1000 births) of babies born to parents in social class V (unskilled manual workers) is more than three times that of babies born to parents in social class I (professionals). This ratio has remained unchanged since the social class groupings were devised in 1911. The infant mortality rate of children born into families of social class V is twice that of children born into professional families, and the chances of being killed by a motor vehicle is five times greater for children from social class V families (Child Accident Prevention Trust, 1989).

Social environment also affects intelligence and growth, although little is known as to how much each of the factors that make up social class differences — wealth, education, nutrition, housing, family relationships, etc. — influence the outcome. In practical terms, doctors and other child health workers should be aware that a pathology may have a specific environmental basis, for example the association of poor housing conditions and respiratory disease.

Common causes of death in childhood

Neonatal period
• Complications of prematurity, including intraventricular haemorrhage
• Congenital abnormalities
• Infection

1–12 months
• Ill defined conditions (including cot death)
• Respiratory infection (pneumonia, etc.)
• Congenital abnormalities (heart disease, etc.)

1–4 years
• Accidents
• Congenital abnormalities
• Respiratory disease

5–14 years
• Accidents
• Cancer
• Congenital abnormalities

15–34 years
• Accidents
• Cancer
• Suicide

2.2   Antenatal and perinatal prevention of death and handicap

Congenital abnormalities

The terms inherited, hereditary, and genetic are used interchangeably to imply conditions that are dependent on genes for their expression.

'Congenital' simply means present at birth and is not synonymous with 'genetic'. Genetic factors may or may not be primarily responsible for producing congenital malformations or abnormalities. An example where genetic factors are not responsible is the congenital malformation resulting from taking thalidomide during pregnancy.

'Familial' is a term used in connection with disorders that occur in aggregation within families but may not have been proved to have a genetic basis (for example diabetes).

Genetic counselling involves advising a family of the risk of their having a baby with an inherited abnormality. It is usually carried out by a specialist in genetics. However, doctors and child health care workers should be aware of the basic information shown in Tables 2.1–2.6.

Antenatal and postnatal screening for congenital abnormalities

Some congenital abnormalities can be diagnosed by tests done before the birth of the child. Many of these tests are only done

Table 2.1 Risk of Down's syndrome with increasing maternal age

Maternal age (years)	Risk of first child being affected
15–19	1 in 1850
20–24	1 in 1600
25–29	1 in 1350
30–34	1 in 800
35–39	1 in 260
40–44	1 in 100
45–49	1 in 50

Table 2.2 Birth frequencies of some dominant conditions in European-derived populations (per 1000 live births)

Huntington's chorea	0.5
Neurofibromatosis	0.4
Myotonic dystrophy	0.2
Multiple polyposis coli	0.1
Polycystic disease of kidneys	0.8
Diaphyseal aclasia	0.5
Dominant forms of blindness	0.1
Dominant forms of early childhood-onset deafness	0.1
Dominant otosclerosis (adult-onset)	1.0
Monogenic hypercholesterolaemia	2.0
Dentinogenesis imperfecta	0.1
Congenital spherocytosis	0.2
Turner's syndrome	0.4

Table 2.3 Birth frequencies of some recessive conditions in UK (per 1000 live births)

Cystic fibrosis	0.5
Phenylketonuria (classic)	0.1
Neurogenic muscle atrophies	0.1
Sickle cell anaemia	0.1
Adrenal hyperplasia	0.1
Severe congenital deafness	0.2
Recessive forms of blindness	0.1
Non-specific recessive forms of severe mental retardation (IQ<50)	0.5

Table 2.4 Birth frequencies in males of sex-linked recessive conditions in European-derived populations (per 1000 live births)

Duchenne's muscular dystrophy	0.2
Haemophilia (classic)	0.1
Ichthyosis (X-linked form)	0.1
Non-specific X-linked forms of mental retardation	0.1

Table 2.5 Effects of drugs on the foetus

Drug	Possible effects on the foetus
Alcohol (in very large amounts)	Fetal alcohol syndrome: slow growth, mental deficiency, facial abnormalities
Androgens and progestogens	Virilization in female foetus. Neoplasm in vagina (not manifest until adolescence)
Antineoplastic drugs	Deformities
Antithyroid drugs	Goitre, hypothyroidism
Chloroquine	Deafness, corneal opacities
Corticosteroids	Adrenal atrophy
Cortisone	Cleft palate
Fertility drugs	Chromosomal aberrations
Folic acid antagonists	Deformities
Rifampicin	Neural tube defect
Streptomycin	Deafness
Sulphonylureas	Hypoglycaemia
Tetracycline	Discoloration of teeth
Warfarin	Nasal bone hypoplasia

No drugs should be given to pregnant women unless absolutely necessary. If in doubt whether a drug has an adverse effect, seek advice, ideally from a hospital pharmacologist.

where there is a high risk of a child having a rare abnormality. Advances in genetic research now make it possible to identify whether either parent carries a defective gene which could cause, for example, sickle cell anaemia or thalassaemia. Within the next few years, the carrier status for other conditions such as cystic fibrosis may also be established. The more routine tests are listed in Table 2.7. Amniocentesis is performed at 15–16 weeks gestation. It is performed under continuous ultrasonographic control and carries a risk of miscarriage of about 1 in 240.

Chorionic villus sampling is undertaken in the first trimester under direct ultrasonographic control. Diagnosis in the first trimester permits simple aspiration methods of termination. Although data is not complete, the risk would appear to be 2%, and may be no greater than for amniocentesis.

Table 2.6 Increase in risk of certain multifactorial conditions when first degree relatives are affected

	Incidence for general population (%)	Incidence for first degree relative when one individual affected (%)	Incidence for first degree relative when two first degree relatives affected (%)
Common congenital defects			
Cleft lip and/or palate	0.1	2–5	9
Club foot	0.1	2–5	10–25
Congenital heart disease	0.5	2–5	10–25
Mental retardation (IQ<70)	2	6	10–20
Neural tube defect (anencephaly, spina bifida, meningomyelocele)	0.2	2–6	10
Congenital dislocation of hip	0.2 in girls 0.025 in boys	5 in girls 0.8 in boys	
Common diseases of postnatal life			
Allergies	18	40	
Cancer	5	5–100	
Diabetes	1–5	5–15	10–40
Hypertension	4–20	20–100	
Schizophrenia	1	7–15	40
Seizures	0.5	3.5	10–15

Table 2.7 Some diseases which can be diagnosed antenatally

Abnormality	Test	Optimal timing of test
Anencephaly and spina bifida	Alphafetoprotein level in blood, followed if necessary by an Amniocentesis	14–18 weeks after conception
		14–18 weeks after conception
Congenital rubella	Blood test for antibodies (not universal)	If contact or disease suspected separated tests to show rise in antibody levels
Cytomegalovirus infection	Blood test for antibodies	If disease suspected
Down's syndrome (in mothers aged over 35–40 years)	Amniocentesis	14–18 weeks after conception
Herpes simplex	Blood test for antibodies	If disease suspected
Rhesus isoimmunization	Blood tests	At regular intervals during pregnancy if suspected
Sex-linked inherited diseases (where specific indications)	Amniocentesis	14–18 weeks after conception
Syphilis	Routine blood test	At booking
Toxoplasmosis	Blood test for antibodies (in endemic areas only)	At booking, and later to check rising antibody levels

More than 30 different diseases can now be diagnosed ante-natally, though most of them are so rare as to make routine screening impractical.

Other specific congenital abnormalities can be diagnosed only by routine testing after birth.

Table 2.8 Common screening tests on the newborn

Abnormality	Test	Timing of test
Routine in all areas		
Phenylketonuria (incidence 1:10 000)	Guthrie test or fluorimetric method on blood, usually taken from heel prick	6−7 days after birth
Recommended for all areas		
Congenital hypothyroidism (incidence 1:3500)	Test for T4 or thyroid stimulating hormone (TSH) done on same sample of blood taken for Guthrie	6−7 days after birth
Recommended for Afro-Caribbean and Mediterranean communities		
Sickle cell disease and thalassaemia	Blood test — electrophoresis	2−7 days after birth

Diseases which can be diagnosed by screening the newborn
The number of screening tests done on newborn babies for
inborn errors of metabolism and other abnormalties varies from
one area to another, according to research interests and labora-
tory facilities. Table 2.8 shows three of the most common tests
carried out in the UK.

2.3 Family planning

Family planning is an integral part of child health care by offering
advice and treatment to prevent unwanted pregnancies occurring.
Free contraceptive advice and services are available from GPs,
family planning clinics, maternity hospitals, young people's advisory clinics, domiciliary services and voluntary organizations such
as the FPA and Brook Advisory Centres. These services are
available for both sexes, and the main object of the professionals
involved is to help the individual or couple to choose the method
of contraception most suitable to them at that particular stage of

their lives, and to ensure that its use is as trouble-free as possible.

The legal aspects of family planning

The 1969 Family Law Reform Act (Section 8) gives young people of 16 and over the right to consent to surgical, medical and dental treatment in the UK without parental consent. A person of 16 years of age and over has the right to professional confidentiality and can decide whether anyone else may be told. This holds for the regulations relating to the Abortion Act of 1967.

Contraceptive advice and treatment for young people under 16

The following guidance results from a review of Section G of the Memorandum of Guidance on the Family Planning Service as specified in the Appendix to HN(81)5 and LASSL(81)2, in the light of the House of Lord's decision in the case of Gillick v. West Norfolk and Wisbech Area Health Authority and the DHSS delivered in October 1983.

1 Both doctors and professional staff should ensure that parental responsibility is not undermined, and to that effect must always seek to encourage either the young person to tell the parents or guardian, or to let them be told.

2 Where this is not possible, for example where family relationships have broken down, then advice and treatment is justified without parental knowledge or consent, providing that:

    (a) the young person understood the advice and was mature enough to understand the moral, social and emotional implications.

    (b) it was impossible to persuade the young person either to inform or to allow the parents to be informed

    (c) the young person would be likely to begin or continue to have unprotected sexual intercourse

    (d) the young person's physical and/or mental health would suffer without advice or treatment

    (e) it was in the young person's best interests to give advice and treatment.

2.4 Accident prevention

Accidents are the most common cause of death in children aged 1–14 years (Tables 2.9–2.11). Overall the most common cause of death is being hit by a motor vehicle, but the majority of injuries for children under 3 occur in the home. Child accidents result in 700 deaths, 120 000 hospital admissions and about 2 million casualty department attendances in England and Wales annually. As a result 10 000 children are permanently disabled each year.

Safety advice to parents

Many accidents can be prevented by taking sensible precautions within the home, parents remaining alert and vigilant, and education of children. Safety advice is an important part of health education. GPs, health visitors and other health care workers should be aware of these safety precautions.

Burns and scalds

The majority of scalds are caused by hot drinks

- Never drink anything hot with a child on your lap or pass hot liquids which may spill over a child's head. A cup of tea/coffee can still scald after 20 minutes
- Kettle flexes should be short/coiled, or cordless
- Kettles and teapots should be kept out of reach, and kettles should not be left simmering. Kettle guards are available. A kettle which has boiled can still scald after 90 minutes
- Buy children's clothes and furniture which are fire resistant
- Keep matches and lighters away from children. A child from about 2 years is able to strike matches and light a lighter
- Fires must be kept guarded. This is a legal requirement when a child is under 12
- Smoke detectors should be fitted in strategic places to alert families to the risk of fire
- Irons should be turned off immediately after use and should be put somewhere safe to cool off. Flexes should not be left dangling
- Handles of all cooking pots should be turned inwards and be aware that cooker guards can get hot

Table 2.9 Accidental deaths by cause, age and sex, England and Wales, 1984

	0–4		5–9		10–14		All ages		
	M	F	M	F	M	F	M	F	Both
Road accidents	57	32	105	57	129	68	291	157	448
Fires	34	19	13	9	8	6	55	34	89
Drownings	27	9	13	0	10	5	50	14	64
Inhalation and ingestion	23	21	3	1	4	0	30	22	52
Falls	20	6	12	1	17	2	49	9	58
Mechanical suffocation	16	12	1	1	19	0	36	13	49
Electrocution	0	1	4	0	3	2	7	3	10
Poisoning — medicine	4	4	0	0	0	1	4	5	9
Poisoning — other	1	2	1	0	12	0	14	6	20
Scalds	5	3	1	0	0	0	6	3	9
Other accidents	25	15	15	2	16	9	56	26	82
All accidents	212	124	168	73	218	95	598	292	890
Fatalities per 10000 population	1.32	0.81	1.12	0.52	1.20	0.55	1.22	0.63	0.93

Source: OPCS Mortality Statistics: Cause 1984. London: HMSO, 1985

• Cold water should be put into the bath first to avoid scalding, and the temperature checked before the child gets in

• Never position objects which attract children on or above fireplaces as clothes may ignite

• Keep a fire extinguisher or fire blanket in the kitchen

Choking/suffocation

• Do not prop feed babies

• Examine toys for loose buttons, eyes, etc. which could be swallowed, and do not let toddlers play with small objects which could cause choking

• Small, hard pieces of food such as peanuts should not be fed to toddlers

• Never use a pillow for a baby

• Keep plastic bags away from children, and ensure that toddlers do not tear apart disposable nappies, bibs, etc. and put bits in their mouths

Falls and cuts

• Fit safety catches on upstairs windows, and window bars if necessary: these should be easily removable in the event of fire

• Position chairs and other furniture away from windows

• Use safety gates on stairs at the top and the bottom, and do not climb over them

• Never leave babies on work surfaces or beds, or in bouncing cradles on work surfaces or table tops

• Make sure stairways are well lit, and that carpets are secure

• Never let children run round with things in their mouths

• All low-level glass in doors, windows or coffee tables should be made from safety glass or covered with adhesive protective safety film

• Encourage children to put their toys away

• In flats with balconies, keep the doors to balconies locked

• Never allow small children to carry breakable objects

• Sweep up (never pick up) broken glass

• Keep knives, scissors, razors and razor blades away from

Table 2.10 Typical pattern of child development and accidents by age

Age	Skills achieved	Falls	Cuts	Burns & scalds	Ingestion inhalation suffocation
All				Conflagration • Smoke detector • Firedrill • Electrical safety Scalds	
Birth		Dropping baby on flat and on stairs		Hot feeds Hot bath water	Proper feeding Open weave clothing Pillows and duvets Plastic in crib
3 months	Wriggles and kicks	From raised surface, e.g. beds			Entrapment — gaps (head) (limbs)
5 months	Rolls over Reaches for objects and grasps Puts objects in mouth	Avoid baby walkers	Sharp objects Ground level	Avoid baby walkers, cups, hot foods	Small parts and items — pins, buttons, Choking on food
8 months	Crawling Manipulation — open/shut push/pull fill/empty poke/ bite/twist Sits unaided	From top of stairs		Contact burns Guards around heaters Flame resistant nightwear	
9 months	Pincer grip Pulls to stand	Out of buggies, highchairs		No table cloths Use mats Flexes (scalds, contact burns)	Wadding — nappies bibs
10 months	Walks holding onto furniture	Over/onto ground and objects	Sharp edged furniture		
11 months	Knows items exist when they are out of sight				Opens lids looks for objects Choking — hard sweets, nuts

Poisons	Road safety	Outdoor play toys	Water	Other
	Adults as role model: • Restraints • Pedestrian safety (use harnesses)			
Accidental poisoning by sibling/parent	Rearward facing infant carrier in car	• Smooth • Too large to swallow • Not furry • No long strings/cords	Drowning in bath	Family dog
Household products and medicines left exposed	Gates to prevent access to street			
	Second stage seat in car			
Opens lids, looks for objects				

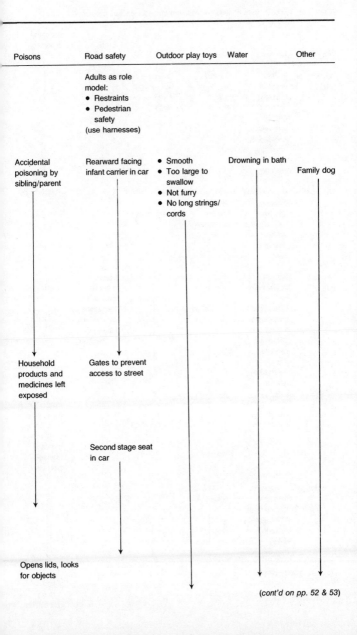

(cont'd on pp. 52 & 53)

Table 2.10 Typical pattern of child development and accidents by age (*cont'd*)

Age	Skills achieved	Falls	Cuts	Burns & scalds	Ingestion inhalation suffocation
13 months	Walks unaided Crawling upstairs Can do — switches/ knobs/dials Interest in hidden objects	Stairs — climbs up then falls	Sharps — table height Architectural glass		
18 months	Imitative play Exploring Climbing furniture, e.g. ladders Emptying/ filling	Off e.g. windows, balconies, bannisters	Sharps — any level — in drawers too		Plastic bags
2 years	Screws beyond one turn Fascinated by smell/taste/ texture Climbs up — can't get down — not deterred by heights			Uses matches/ lighters Turns taps by self (reduce tapwater temperature)	
3 years pre-school	Stops putting objects into mouth		Tools and sharps in garden shed		Now acceptable to have parts in toys/games still can't manage peanuts
Pre-school	Competent on stairs Climbs trees Manipulates — cogs/nuts/ bolts Popping tubes				

Source: CAPT, 1989

Poisons	Road safety	Outdoor play toys	Water	Other
May open household chemical containers without child-resistant closures	Pedestrian safety-harnesses	Can now cope with sit-on toddle trucks	Drowning, e.g. garden	
May open medicines without child-resistant closures		Garden play equipment surfaces underneath		Next sibling
May open child-resistant closures	Pedestrian safety education starts here	Tricycles Can't use brakes		
	Third stage car restraint	Can use simple battery operated ride-ons OK from 4 Footbrakes from 5		

Table 2.11 Fatal accidents by age and sex. England and Wales, 1987

| | 0–4 Years | | 5–14 Years | | Total | | |
	Boys	Girls	Boys	Girls	Boys	Girls	Both
Transport accidents	61	37	184	99	245	136	381 (55%)
Home accidents	95	57	28	17	123	74*	197 (29%)
Other accidents	31	13	46	17	78*	32*	110 (16%)

* includes age not known cases
Source: OPCS. Deaths by accidents and violence. Quarterly Monitors DH4 Series. London: OPCS, 1988.

small children, and teach older children to carry knives and scissors correctly. Catches are available for drawers, fridges and freezers
• Small fingers can be easily crushed in doors

Gardens, DIY and outdoor safety for children
• Weedkillers and other garden chemicals must be kept in clearly marked containers out of reach and sight of children
• Garden gates should be fitted with a childproof catch
• Never leave garden tools lying around, and put tools away after use — children try to mimic adults using equipment
• Never leave electric mowers or other electrical DIY equipment plugged in when unattended. Use residual circuit breakers (RCB) for all such equipment
• Keep ponds fenced or covered when children are young
• Swimming or paddling pools should be securely covered when an adult is not around to supervise
• When leaving a baby in a pram in the garden, cover it with a cat net
• Cover sandpits to prevent fouling by animals; any animal excreta deposited in the garden should be removed or dug well in

- Supervise small children in playgrounds, especially on or around swings
- Use proper ramps for cars, not piles of bricks
- Keep children away when sanding, grinding or spraying: in one-third of all DIY accidents it is the watching child who is hurt
- Ensure that ladders have a firm footing and do not let children climb them

Poisoning

Accidental poisoning occurs almost totally in the pre-school age child (see Fig. 2.1). Incidents tend to occur at times when parents are stressed, such as moving house or returning from holidays.

In many cases first-line treatment of poisoning can be carried out by inducing vomiting. Because of this it is useful for the GP to

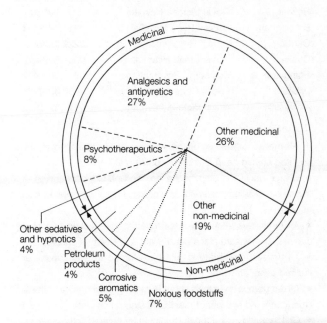

Fig. 2.1 Substances known to have caused poisoning in children aged 0–14 years admitted to hospital.

have Ipecacuanha handy at all times. Any queries concerning poisoning are best answered by reference to the poison centres (telephone numbers below), but emergency cases should always be referred to hospital casualty departments immediately.

Do not cause the child to vomit when he/she is unconscious; or when he/she has swallowed corrosives (alkalis or acids), petroleum distillates or strychnine.

Telephone numbers of poison centres
Further information regarding the dangers and treatment of poisoning can be obtained round the clock from these centres.

London	Guy's Hospital	071 635 9191
		071 407 7600
Belfast	Royal Victoria Hospital	0232 240503
Birmingham	Dudley Road Hospital	021 554 3801
Cardiff	Cardiff Royal Infirmary	0222 709901
Dublin	Jervis Street Hospital	0001 379966
Edinburgh	Edinburgh Royal Infirmary	031 229 2477
Leeds	Leeds General Infirmary	0532 430715
Newcastle	Royal Victoria Infirmary	091 232 1525

• All medicines, either on prescription or purchased over the counter, should be in childproof containers
• Blister packs or strip packs are acceptable alternatives, if stored out of sight and reach, as a child is unlikely to swallow a lot at once
• All medicines should be kept together in a locked medicine cabinet, or in a safe place out of sight and reach of children
• All unused medicines should be returned to a pharmacy or flushed away down the lavatory
• All dangerous chemicals should be kept in their original bottles, clearly marked and out of reach and sight of children
• Children's toys and furniture should be painted with non-toxic paint

• Remember elderly relatives may keep medicines in their own homes by bedsides or in handbags

Toxicity of common household items and drugs

Aeroplane glues   act as a mild irritant if ingested or squirted into the eyes. Only harmful if inhaled in large quantities as in 'glue sniffing'

Alcohol   may cause intoxication and hypoglycaemia. Unless quantities are small refer to hospital

Anti-diarrhoea medicines   many of these are potentially dangerous; in case of doubt, contact a poison centre

Aspirin   (salicylates) refer to hospital children who have swallowed anything more than the therapeutic dose

Ball pen contents   are harmless

Batteries   (dry cell) contain mercuric chloride, which is toxic, but five complete batteries need to be ingested before the lethal dose is reached. Other batteries contain acids which may cause burns; if in doubt refer to hospital

Bleaches   may be solutions of hypochlorites, which are corrosive — refer to hospital

Bubble bath soaps   are detergents and may occasionally cause vomiting — no need to refer

Candles   are beeswax or paraffin and are not likely to cause symptoms

Caps for toy pistols   — even a complete roll is non-toxic

Cigarettes   a child eating a cigarette or cigar usually vomits, initially due to absorption of nicotine from the stomach; this removes part of the tobacco. If more than one is ingested, refer to hospital

Cologne, perfumes and after-shave lotions   contain alcohol and can cause intoxication and hypoglycaemia. If more than a very small quantity has been swallowed, refer to hospital

Contraceptives   (oral) no specific treatment required. Girls occasionally get withdrawal bleeding

Crayons   non-toxic

Detergents are mild gastric irritants and may cause vomiting. No treatment required

Drain cleaners are caustic alkalis and cause burns of mouth, pharynx and oesophagus. Urgent hospital treatment required

Dry cleaning fluid may contain carbon tetrachloride or trichlorethylene, both of which are toxic. Refer to hospital

Felt tipped pens non-toxic

Iron tablets, or vitamin tablets containing iron even small amounts of iron are toxic to children and hospitalization should be immediate

Lavatory deodorizing cakes contain *p*-dichlorobenzene, or less commonly naphthalene. Both require hospital treatment

Lead whether ingested or inhaled (burning car batteries), requires urgent hospital treatment

Lighter fuel may cause intoxication pneumonia. Refer to hospital

Matches are relatively non-toxic, but large quantities may cause sore mouth and vomiting

Marking, indelible or special purpose inks some of these contain aniline dyes or other toxic substances; cases should be referred to hospital

Nail varnish usually contains acetone, which is toxic. Refer to hospital

Paints almost universally non-toxic, but old paints and some red paints may contain lead

Paint removers are usually strong alkalis, causing burns of mouth, pharynx and oesophagus. Refer urgently to hospital

Paraffin can cause increasing unconsciousness and/or pneumonia. Refer to hospital

Paraquat is lethal and cases of ingestion need urgent referral to hospital

Petrol causes central nervous system depression and pneumonia. Refer to hospital

Pencils are non-toxic — 'lead' pencils do not contain lead

Play-dough is edible, digestible, non-toxic

Putty ingestion of less than 100 grams should do no harm. More than this may cause mechanical obstruction

Shampoo   see bubble bath soaps

Soaps   may cause mild vomiting — no need to refer

Silly putty   is non-toxic

Thermometers   the broken glass may cut the mouth but the amount of mercury present is not harmful even if swallowed

When sending a child to hospital with suspected or definite poisoning always arrange for the container of the poison to go too

Some poisonous plants and fungi

Poisoning by plants and berries is extremely rare, with only three recorded deaths between 1958 and 1977.

Berries   many berries are brightly coloured and attractive to children. Some can be fatal, such as holly, spindle, etc.

Cuckoo pint/Lords and Ladies   the leaves are toxic and the red/orange berries are poisonous

Daffodil   ingestion of the bulb can cause nausea and vomiting

Hemlock   the whole plant is poisonous

Laburnum   commonly believed to be highly poisonous, but in fact only causes gastric upsets

Laurel   causes vomiting, convulsions, slow pulse, low blood pressure. Hospital treatment is urgently required

Lily of the Valley   all parts are toxic including the water in which cut flowers stand

Lupin   is poisonous and can cause paralysis, depressed respiration and convulsions. Hospital treatment is required

Morning Glory   the seeds contain LSD which can cause permanent brain damage

Mushrooms   wild mushrooms should never be eaten unless expert advice is obtained first. If in doubt about a mushroom that has already been ingested, try to obtain a sample and seek advice from a hospital

Nightshade (blue or black)   both the leaves and the fruit are poisonous, causing abdominal pain, vomiting, diarrhoea, respiratory depression and shock. Urgent hospital treatment is required

Rhododendron is poisonous and can cause vomiting, convulsions, lowered blood pressure and paralysis. Hospital treatment is urgent

Rhubarb the leafy part contains oxalic acid which can cause nausea, vomiting, diarrhoea, haemorrhages. Seek hospital treatment

Sweet peas are poisonous and can cause paralysis, convulsions, and depressed breathing. Hospital treatment is urgent

Wisteria can cause gastric upset, usually not severe

Yew the wood, bark, leaves and seeds are all poisonous and cause nausea, vomiting, diarrhoea, abdominal pain, dilated pupils, weakness, shock. Hospital treatment is urgently required

---

When sending a child to hospital with suspected or definite poisoning always arrange for a specimen of the plant or fungus to go too

Road traffic accidents

More than half the children accidentally killed each year die as a result of a road traffic accident (RTA). Within this group the majority (60%) will die as pedestrians, 20% as car occupants and 15% as cyclists.

● Teach children the Green Cross Code by example as well as instruction

● Teach children from an early age to be aware of road hazards

● Children should not be allowed to cross major roads alone under the age of 10

● Children's bikes should be checked regularly for defective brakes, lights, tyres, and reflectors

● Wearing reflective clothing and crash helmets should be encouraged

Safety in cars

Since seat belt legislation in cars was introduced in 1983, there has been a 25% fall in deaths and serious injuries to front seat passengers, although this has had only a small effect on deaths and injuries to children as most children travel in the back seat. In 1989 further legislation was introduced which states

1 Everyone travelling in the front seat of a car must wear a seat belt

2 Children under 1 year must use a restraint system (see Table 2.12) appropriate for their age — a rearward facing infant carrier or a properly restrained carrycot if either is available

3 Children between 1 and 4 years old must use a restraint designed for their size and weight, or an adult belt with a booster cushion, if either is fitted

4 Children from 4 to 14 years old travelling in the back of a car must use a restraint specifically designed for them or an adult seat belt, if either is available

5 It is illegal to carry a child on your lap in the front seat

6 It is illegal to use a restraint for more than one person

General points

• Use child locks on rear doors

• Never leave a child in a closed car in the summer, as it can easily overheat

• Unattended cars should be left locked, and children never allowed to play in them

• Before reversing always check a child's whereabouts

The safest way of carrying children in cars is:

(a) in a restraint suitable to the child's age and size in the back seat; or

(b) an infant rear facing car seat in the front passenger seat; or

(c) in an adult seat belt in the front seat with a booster cushion if possible (not suitable for infants under 4 years); or

(d) unrestrained in the back seat — *but only as a last resort*

See Table 2.12 for approved child restraints.

Table 2.12 Child restraint systems

Approximate age and size of child	Type of restraint and Standard*	Position in car
0–9 months Less than 20 lbs (9 kg). Until the child can sit up unaided	Babyseat BS AU202 Carrycot in a harness (BS AU186)	Rear facing and on the rear seat. *Not* in the rear compartment of hatchback and estate cars
9 months–4 years 20–40 lbs (9–18 kg)	Child safety seat (BS 3254, ECE Reg 44)	Rear seat
5–9 years 40–80 lbs (18–36 kg)	Adult seat belt with booster cushion (BS AU185, ECE Reg 44) *or* child harness (BS 3254)	Preferably in the rear seat Rear seat
10 years and above	Adult seat belt (BS 3254, ECE Reg 16)	Preferably in the rear seat

* Approved restraints have either the British Standard Institution's Kitemark and carry a BS number or a European approval symbol:

BSI kitemark   European approval symbols

It is important that the long term consequences of road traffic accidents are considered. Although the outcome of injuries is generally a full recovery, 5% experience some form of permanent disability, such as brain damage, limb deformity or permanent scarring. More important, perhaps, are the long term psychological or personality changes which may occur.

2.5 Sudden infant death

Detailed research in many different areas, such as epidemiology and genetics, has identified the causes of most deaths in childhood. However, one baby in every 500 live births dies unexpectedly and unexplainedly between the age of 1 week and 2 years. The majority of these children will die before the age of 8 months (90%), with a peak between 2 to 4 months (40%). Recent studies have shown that there may be an associated risk between sleeping position and sudden infant death syndrome (SIDS). It is therefore advised that babies be put to sleep on alternating sides, with the lower elbow a little in front of the body.

Certain factors seem to be associated with an increased incidence of sudden infant death, and these include

- Social class IV and V
- Smoking during pregnancy
- Young, single unsupported mothers
- Families with low paid or unemployed breadwinner
- Male infants
- Winter months (see Fig. 2.2)
- Low birth weight

Scoring systems, such as the Sheffield Multistage Scoring System and the Relative Risks system devised by the Foundation for the Study of Infant Deaths, may determine those at high risk. Until causative factors are better understood and can be properly prevented, however, the main concern of doctors and health care workers must be to help the families cope with their grief.

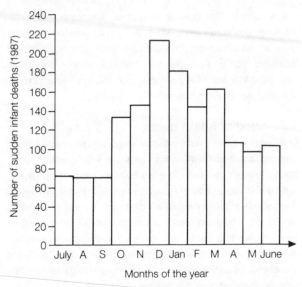

Fig. 2.2 Number of sudden infant deaths by month of year for 1987 (total 1528). (Foundation for the Study of Infant Deaths, March 1989.)

Some questions frequently asked by parents of children who have died unexpectedly, with suggested replies:

Why did the baby die?
In some cases when a baby dies suddenly at home, the post mortem reveals a previously unsuspected abnormality or evidence of a rapidly fatal infectious disease, such as pneumonia or meningitis. In the majority of cases, however, although there may be signs of a mild infection, the post mortem findings do not explain the child's death.

Could anything have been done to prevent it happening?
Cot death by its very nature cannot be foreseen by parents, doctors, health visitors or anyone else. However parents, siblings

and others connected with the family are often left with a great feeling of guilt and they will need to talk about this.

Does the baby suffer?

Most of these babies die in their sleep. Even if not asleep, it appears that they become unconscious and die rapidly. There is no indication that they suffer any pain or distress.

Did the baby suffocate?

These babies are sometimes found in the cot with the blankets over their faces. Many normal babies sleep face down or get the blankets over their faces with no harmful effects.

Did the baby choke or vomit on his/her last feed?

Sometimes vomit or blood-tinged froth is found around the baby's mouth or on the bedding. This occurs during or even after death but does not cause the death.

Is the condition infectious or contagious?

The condition is not infectious or contagious and is not transmitted to other members of the family.

Does breastfeeding protect against cot death?

At the moment there is no definite answer to this question. Cot deaths do occur in breastfed babies but may be less common.

Why do the coroner and the police investigate the baby's death?

It is the duty of the coroner to investigate all sudden death where there is no obvious cause. They are aided in this by the police. In Scotland these deaths may be investigated by the Procurator Fiscal.

What about future babies?

The risk of the same happening to another baby in the family is extremely remote. However parents may well want to talk to the family doctor or to a specialist to gain further reassurance.

Further information and a leaflet for the parents of a child who has died suddenly and unexpectedly in infancy can be obtained from the Foundation for the Study of Infant Deaths, 5th Floor, 4–5 Grosvenor House, London SW1X 7HD, telephone 071–235 1721.

Checklist for GP/Community Doctor/Health Visitor, after an unexpected infant death

The following notes are intended to help doctors/health visitors managing a cot death for the first time.

As soon as you hear of the baby's death, *contact the family* to express sympathy, by a home visit if possible. Early support prevents later misunderstandings.

Unless there is obvious injury, a history of illness or the parental attitude arouses suspicion, tell the parents it appears to be a cot death but that a post mortem examination will be necessary to clarify the cause of death. If the death remains unexplained, it may be registered as 'sudden infant death syndrome'. Some parents or older siblings want to see or hold their child after it has died but before the body is taken to a mortuary.

Explain the Coroner's duty and the possibility of an inquest, and warn parents that they or relatives may be asked to identify the body. Advise the parents that they will be asked to make a statement to the Coroner's office or police, and that bedding may be taken for examination to help establish the cause of death. If necessary, give advice on registering the death and making funeral arrangements. The Coroner's office may need to know the parents' choice of burial or cremation.

If the mother was breastfeeding, she will need advice on suppression of lactation.

Take particular note of siblings. Remember that a surviving twin carries extra risk of cot death and may need careful observation. Give guidance on emotional needs of siblings, who may be neglected or over-protected; reassure parents that older children are not a risk.

Advise parents of likely grief reactions such as aching arms, hearing the baby cry, distressing dreams, and strong positive or negative sexual feelings, but reassure them that these and other symptoms such as loss of appetite and sleeplessness are normal and temporary. Anger, sometimes directed towards the GP, guilt and self-blame, especially on the part of the mother, are common grief reactions for which the doctor should be prepared.

Offer parents copies of the leaflet *Information For The Parents Of A Child Who Has Died Suddenly And Unexpectedly In Infancy* (obtainable from the Foundation for the Study of Infant Deaths, whose address is given above).

Make sure that parents have a relative or close friend very near them during the 48 hours after the death, and offer explanations to them and to the minister of religion, if any. Make sure the family's health visitor and other members of the primary care team know of the baby's death and are prepared to give continued support.

Arrange a subsequent meeting with the parents to discuss the cause of death. Make sure the Coroner informs you of the initial and final post mortem findings and consult with the pathologist if any clarification is needed.

Offer a later interview with a paediatrician, both for parents and the siblings. An independent opinion is mutually beneficial to the parents and GP as it restores parental confidence in the primary care team and shares some of the load of counselling, particularly concerning future children.

Parents who have lost a baby unexpectedly will need extra attention and support with their subsequent children from their obstetrician, paediatrician, general practitioner and health visitor.

The grief of parents

The pain experienced by parents following the death of a child is described as the most intense ever suffered. The first reaction is of shock, disbelief, denial or numbness. Feelings of guilt, anger and frustration are commonly experienced, with crying offering release from these feelings. Sharing and talking about these feelings with someone who really cares can help, but some people, especially men, may experience difficulties. Relatives and friends may be uncomfortable with death, and help may be obtained from clergymen, physicians, counsellors, health visitors, and other bereaved parents. Although the lost child is never forgotten, the painful days do become less frequent.

The grief of children

Children cannot be protected from the reality of death, but it is even harder to explain an unexpected death, especially when the parents are in the midst of their own grief. They should be allowed to participate in the rituals related to death, and will be helped to understand and cope with death as well as finding comfort within a loving, supportive network. For children whose reaction seems to be prolonged, or for parents who find the situation difficult, professional advice can be helpful.

Care of next infant (CONI)

For a family who has suffered the tragedy of a cot death, it is inevitable that the next pregnancy and the early months of the new baby's life will be a time of great anxiety. It is important that every family should receive adequate support with a subsequent pregnancy and until the baby is beyond the cot death period.

Suggested methods of support

• Regular weekly contact with an informed health visitor, the support of a knowledgeable GP and ready access to a paediatrician with special interest in cot death

• Symptom diaries to allow parents to express and discuss anxieties about illness

• Weighing babies — daily or regular weighing, perhaps by the parents at home, with the weights recorded on the Sheffield Weight Chart

• Apnoea monitors. These do not guarantee the prevention of death and intervention may or may not be successful. Parents should discuss their own and their baby's needs as to the most suitable monitor. Training in resuscitation methods should be given and proper back up support available

• Monitoring of environmental temperature. Both excessive heat or cold have been shown to be dangerous, and monitoring may be helpful

2.6   Child abuse

The law recognizes two types of abuse — physical and sexual. Physical abuse may take the form of carelessness, neglect or deliberately inflicted injury or poisoning. It should be suspected when the explanation of an injury is inadequate or discrepant, or when it is known or suspected that an injury was inflicted or knowingly not prevented.

Sexual abuse may be defined as the involvement of children or adolescents in sexual activities that they do not comprehend, to which they are unable to give their consent, or which violate the social and legal taboos of society.

Factors which may be associated with an increased incidence of child abuse:

Although child abuse occurs in all socioeconomic classes, there are predisposing factors in cases of child abuse.

• Poor socioeconomic circumstances
• Birth of first baby to parents under the age of 20
• Stress
• Diffuse social and medical problems which hinder making relationships
• Separation from parents in special care baby units
• Psychiatric illness in mother or disturbed behaviour in hospital, excluding 'baby blues'
• Social, cultural and emotional isolation, i.e. lack of supportive kin, friends or neighbours
• Undiagnosed physical illness in mother or baby
• History of either parent having been abused in childhood
• Marital problems, often with violence

● Unrealistic expectations of child by parents, e.g. social, emotional, developmental, intellectual, behavioural

Physical abuse

Points to explore from the history
● Inadequate or discrepant explanation of the injury
● Delay in taking the child for medical examination
● Frequent visits to the doctor for trivial reasons
● Failure to thrive or signs of neglect in the child
● Disturbed behaviour in the parents
● Previous injury to the child or sibling

Specific points to look for on examination
Bruises
● Any bruises on a baby in the first year, especially when on the cheek or head
● Bruises from adult human bites
● Two black eyes without bruising of the forehead
● 'Purple ear' from bruising, or fading bruising of the ear and surrounding scalp
● Petechial haemorrhages (from rough handling of a young baby) or bizarre marks and bruises of the skin
● 'Finger and thumb' bruises on the face, trunk and limbs, especially on the trunk of a young baby who has been held firmly and shaken

Fracture
● Any fracture in the first year which does not have a history of accident

Burns and scalds
● Circular blebs, sores and scars from cigarette burns are often found in clusters and may be of different ages
● Other burns and scalds in young children should be investi-

gated by taking a detailed history to rule out the possibility that they were deliberately inflicted

Mouth
- If there is a small blood clot on the gum or tongue, examine for a tear of the frenulum or elsewhere in the buccal mucosa (this may be caused by ramming the bottle or fist in the mouth of a crying baby).
- Sundry cuts, scratches, excoriations or sores around the mouth, often of different ages

Poisoning
- Ingestion of tablets, medicines or other 'fluids' may not always be accidental carelessness, although very hard to prove otherwise

Demeanour of baby/child
- Slow, wary responses
- 'Frozen watchfulness'

Sexual abuse
A child making a clear, unambiguous statement about sexual abuse should be taken seriously. Whilst most sexually abused children show no physical evidence, sexual abuse should be *considered* in such conditions as

- Genital trauma, e.g. vulvo-vaginitis associated with soreness and discharge; vaginal bleeding; lacerations or bruising; enlarged vaginal opening or a scarred hymen
- Faecal soiling, retention or rectal bleeding, anal fissures or scars or a lax or pouting anal sphincter
- Sexually transmitted disease, including anal/vaginal warts
- Pregnancy under 16, especially where the identity of the father is vague or secret
- Unexplained emotional disturbance
- Undue sexual awareness or sexual provocativeness
- Running away from home, or self destructive behaviour

The Children Act 1989

The Children Act 1989 is based on the belief that children are best looked after within the family. 'Parental responsibility' is a phrase which is used to define the duties, rights and authority which parents have in respect of their child, and emphasizes the duty to care for and raise the child to moral, physical, and emotional health as the fundamental task of parenthood. Parents retain their parental responsibility even when compulsory powers have been taken by the courts.

It goes on to state that the welfare of children is paramount, and requires that local authorities promote the upbringing of children in need. 'Children in need' are defined as those children requiring services to secure a reasonable standard of health and development, and include children who are disabled (see Chapter 4 p. 114).

The local authority is further required to take reasonable steps to identify those children in need, and to take reasonable steps to prevent neglect or abuse. The aims are to keep vulnerable children out of care, safeguard any passage into care and to protect children who are in care.

Under the 1989 Act, the notion of voluntary care is obsolete, but local authorities are empowered to provide accommodation to children in need when the person caring for the child 'can no longer do so for whatever reason'.

Procedures in cases of child abuse

All UK health districts have written guidelines on child protection procedures.

Any person with knowledge or suspicion that a child is either being abused or is at risk of abuse has a duty to refer their concern to one or more of the agencies with statutory powers of intervention and investigation — the NSPCC, the police or the Social Services Department. All allegations should be treated seriously and investigated as a matter of urgency, especially if made by close relatives, children, or parents referring themselves.

The diagnosis of sexual abuse does not necessarily call for emergency response or removal of a child from the home. It may be more appropriate, for example in cases of incest, for the abuser to be required to live away from home, whilst supporting the family during therapy. The child should not be subjected to repeated medical examinations or interviews.

The investigation of child abuse should be conducted on a multi-agency, multidisciplinary basis, with a pooling of all relevant medical and social assessments and information. If a decision is made for the child's name to be included on the local child protection register (see p. 75), either social services or the NSPCC should carry future child care responsibility for the case. A key worker should be designated to fulfil the statutory responsibilities for the welfare and protection of the child, as well as co-ordinating interagency activity in the case. Reviews should be at agreed intervals to suit the needs of each case, but should take place at least every 6 months.

Openness and honesty are an essential basis for building a foundation of understanding between parents and professionals. Parents need to know the reasons for professional concern and should be informed and consulted at every stage of the investigation. It is recommended that parents be invited to attend part, or if appropriate the whole of case conferences, unless their presence would preclude a full and proper consideration of the child's interests. They should be informed of the outcome of the case conference as soon as is practicable and this should be confirmed in writing.

The welfare of the child must be of immediate concern and an urgent decision made as to whether the child can stay at home, return home or be removed to a place of safety, for example a hospital, either by seeking a child assessment order or an emergency protection order.

The safety of other children in the household should be considered at the same time.

Emergency Protection Order

The purpose of an Emergency Protection Order (EPO) is to protect a child from harm. Whilst no proof of actual harm is necessary, the applicant — usually the social services or the

NSPCC — must satisfy the court that 'there is reasonable cause to believe the child is likely to suffer significant harm.' This is determined by comparison of a child's health and development with what is expected of a similar child. An EPO may be for 8 days or less in the first instance, and can only be extended once for a further period not exceeding 7 days, on application by the social services or the NSPCC.

The police can act in an emergency without a court's authority and take a child into police protection for a maximum of 72 hours. During this time the case must be inquired into by the social services.

Child Assessment Order

A Child Assessment Order (CAO) may be made on application to the court by social services or the NSPCC, with the full knowledge of all parties, when

(a) there is reasonable cause that a child is suffering or is likely to suffer significant harm;

(b) an assessment of the child's health, development or the way he/she has been treated is required to determine whether the child is or is likely to suffer;

(c) an assessment is unlikely to be made without such an order.

The order must specify the date on which the assessment is to begin, and is effective for a maximum of 7 days from that date.

The CAO has been designed to assist local authorities carrying out investigative duties with respect of a child, but where there is no case to warrant an emergency protection order, care or supervision order. The court, however, may decide that an emergency protection order is the more appropriate order.

Care order

A care order commits a child to the care of the local authority, and the child may be placed in residential care, a foster home or back at home. The Act provides for the parents to retain parental responsibility (although the local authority may limit its operation), to be involved with local authority decision making and to have reasonable contact with the child, unless the court decides otherwise.

A care order lasts until the child's 18th birthday but may be discharged earlier on the application of the local authority, the child or any person who has parental responsibility.

Interim care order

The court has the ability to make certain directions, for example medical or social assessments of the child, and the duration of the order is more restricted. The first interim care order cannot last for more than 8 weeks and any later order cannot last for more than 4 weeks. The powers and responsibilities of local authorities for full, interim and supervision orders are the same.

Supervision order

A supervision order places the child under the supervision of a local authority or probation officer. It is the duty of the supervisor to assess, assist and befriend the child. The Act imposes obligations not only on the child but also on a 'responsible person', for example a person who has parental responsibility or with whom the child is living, to inform the supervisor of the child's address and to allow the supervisor reasonable contact. If these requirements are not complied with, a search warrant may be sought.

A supervision order lasts initially for 1 year and application by the supervisor may extend it for up to 3 years. It cannot last beyond the child's 18th birthday and the supervisor is required to consider variation or discharge if it is not complied with in full or if it is deemed no longer necessary.

Child Protection Register

A central register held by the Social Services Department, or the NSPCC on its behalf, should be maintained listing all the children who have been abused or are considered to be at risk of abuse. A child's name should normally only appear following interagency agreement at a case conference. The situation should be reviewed every 6 months, and in the event of a child moving away, the new area should be alerted to place the child's name on the register for that area. An interagency case conference should agree to the removal of a child's name from the register. This does not mean an automatic withdrawal or reduction in services.

After-care

Local authorities are required to advise, assist and befriend each child who has been accommodated in local authority care; by voluntary organizations; in a registered children's home; by health or education authority; residential care, nursing home or mental home for a period of at least 3 months, or privately fostered. Steps should be taken to prepare a child for the time when he or she is no longer being cared for by assistance 'in kind', and in exceptional circumstances, in cash.

Further reading and references

An Introduction to The Children Act 1989, HMSO, London

Child Accident Prevention Trust (1989) *Basic Principles of Child Accident Prevention*, CAPT

DHSS (Revised 1984) *Handbook of Contraceptive Practice*, HMSO, London

DHSS (1987) *Report of the Inquiry into Child Abuse in Cleveland 1987*, HMSO, London

DHSS (1988) *Working Together*, HMSO, London

DoH (1989) *An Introduction to The Children Act 1989*, HMSO, London

Fry J., Hasler J. (1986) *Primary Health Care 2000*, Churchill Livingstone, Edinburgh

Golding J., Limerick S., Macfarlane A. (1985) *Sudden Infant Death, Patterns, Puzzles and Problems*, Open Books, Shepton Mallet

Hall D.M.B. (1989) *Health for all Children*, Oxford University Press, Oxford

Hudson B. (1989) Charter for children, *The Health Service Journal*, Oct., 1283–4

Kempe R.S., Kempe C.H. (1978) *Child Abuse*, Fontana Open Books, London

Loudon N. (1985) *Handbook of Family Planning*, Churchill Livingstone, Edinburgh

OPCS Monitor (1985–87)

Thompson J. (1989) Cot death, *Community Outlook*, Oct. 32–7

Waite A.J. (1988) Managing subsequent siblings of cot death victims, *Health Visitor*, **61**:8, 244–6

3 Health promotion and advice

3.1 Immunization

The World Health Organization (WHO) in its document 'Health for All' has a clearly stated aim that by the year 2000 indigenous poliomyelitis, measles, neonatal tetanus, congenital rubella and diphtheria should have been eradicated from Europe. The DoH has endorsed this statement and further states that no child should be denied immunization without serious thought as to the consequences both for the individual child and the community.

Practical notes on immunization

Consent must be given by the parent or guardian and the child's fitness and suitability for immunization must be established.

Immunization should be delayed if the child is suffering from an acute febrile illness. Minor coughs and colds are not contra-indications.

If a child misses an injection the child should not start the course again but should be immunized at the earliest opportunity. *No opportunity to immunize should be missed.*

No preparation is required for 'socially clean' skin. If alcohol is used it should dry completely before administration of vaccine, otherwise it may inactivate live vaccine.

The anterolateral aspect of the thigh or upper arm is the recommended site for immunization.

Three weeks should elapse between the administration of two live vaccines. Alternatively they may be administered simultaneously in different sites.

Manufacturers' instructions for storage, reconstitution and disposal of unused vaccines must be observed.

Reactions following administration of vaccines should be reported on a yellow card without delay to the Committee on Safety of Medicines.

All immunizations should be accurately recorded for parents and health authority information systems. Complications or reactions should also be recorded.

Immunization by nurses

Doctors may delegate responsibility for immunization to a nurse, either in the clinic, home or elsewhere, providing the following conditions are fulfilled (DHSS, 1988).

1 The nurse is willing to be professionally accountable for this work

2 The nurse has received training and is competent in all aspects of immunizations, including the contraindications to specific vaccines

3 Adequate training has been given in the recognition and treatment of anaphylaxis

Contraindications to the use of live vaccines

1 Live vaccines should not be administered to pregnant women because of the theoretical risk of harm to the foetus. In the event of an epidemic, however, the need for vaccination outweighs the risk

2 Live vaccines should not be administered to the following:

(a) patients receiving high-dose corticosteroid (2 mg/kg/day) until 3 months after cessation of therapy.

(b) patients with impaired immunological mechanism, e.g. hypogammaglobulinaemia.

(c) patients with immunosuppression through disease or therapy, including irradiation, should not receive live vaccine until 6 months after cessation of therapy.

It is essential that children in groups (a), (b) and (c) receive immunoglobulin as soon as possible after exposure to measles or chicken pox. *NB Siblings and close contacts should be fully immunized, although inactivated polio vaccine should replace the live vaccine.*

Specialist opinion may recommend the administration of alternative killed vaccines for these children.

HIV infected children should receive immunization in accordance with the standard schedules (see p. 85). Non-immunized children with asymptomatic AIDS should not receive BCG, but should receive the other vaccines.

Practical notes on specific vaccines

BCG
This may be given to infants aged less than 1 month without prior
tuberculin testing. Vaccination is recommended for all babies
from families with a history or high risk of TB.

Contraindications (see p. 79 for general points)
BCG should not be administered to
• People with positive tuberculin tests above Heaf Grade 2
• People with any generalized septic skin condition
• HIV positive individuals
    No further immunization should be given for at least 3 months
in the arm in which BCG was given, because of the risk of
regional lymphadenitis.

Testing
The Heaf test is performed on the clean dry forearm with a drop of
tuberculin PPD (Protein Purified Derivative) being placed on to
the skin. It is spread into a thin film and the gun fired vertically to
ensure all six needles penetrate equally.
    The test should be read from 3 to 10 days later (Table 3.1).
    It is helpful if the answers to the following questions are
obtained in each case where a positive Heaf Grade 2, 3 or 4 is
reported:
• Has the child ever had BCG? (Check for presence of scar)
• Is there any history of attendance at a Chest Clinic or of
tuberculosis in the family or contacts?
• Has the child ever lived in a country where the incidence of
tuberculosis may be high?

Vaccination with BCG
The vaccine is given with a sterile disposable tuberculin syringe
and needle. Each needle should be used once only. The dried
vaccine should be protected from light and stored between 2° and

Table 3.1 The Heaf test

Result	Action
Negative	
Nothing to see or 0–3 raised papules	Vaccinate with BCG
Positive	
Grade 1: 4+ raised papules	As above
Grade 2: raised red ring with joined papules	Refer for chest X-ray and medical opinion, unless BCG previously given
Grade 3: raised red lump	Refer for chest X-ray and medical opinion
Grade 4: vesiculated red lump	

8° C. Full instructions for the reconstitution of the vaccine are enclosed with each package.

The dose is 0.1 ml (0.05 ml for infants under 3 months of age) given strictly intradermally at the insertion of the deltoid muscle. The anterolateral aspect of the thigh may be used for cosmetic reasons, although this site is unsuitable for infants.

All reconstituted BCG should be discarded at the end of the session.

Measles, mumps and rubella

This replaced measles vaccine in October 1988. In order to achieve the DoH recommendation of 90% uptake by 1990, which aims to eliminate measles, mumps and congenital rubella syndrome, all children between 1 and 5 years are eligible to receive the MMR vaccine. MMR may also be given to children of any age whose parents request it, and to all non-immune adults on prescription. The vaccine should be given soon after the first birthday, irrespective of any delay of DTP.

Measles, mumps and rubella vaccine should be given irrespective of previous measles infection or a history of measles, mumps or rubella infection.

Parents should be given advice on care and treatment of fever in the event of a febrile reaction 5–10 days following immunization. Parotid swelling occasionally occurs, usually in the third week. Post-vaccination symptoms are not infectious.

Immunoglobulin as used with measles vaccine must *not* be given with MMR as it may inhibit the immune response to mumps and rubella.

No child should be refused immunization.

Contraindications (see p. 79 for general points)
Anaphylactic shock reaction to egg is the *only* contraindication to MMR. Dislike of egg or refusal to eat it is not a contraindication.

Pertussis
Neurological complications are considerably more common after the disease than after vaccination. There is no upper age limit for immunization against pertussis.

Contraindications
The only **absolute contraindication** to immunization is a severe local or general reaction to a preceding dose, defined as follows:
• **Local reaction** — redness and swelling greater than half the circumference of the limb which received the injection;
• **General reaction** — fever of 39.5°C or more within 48 hours of immunization; generalized collapse; prolonged inconsolable screaming; convulsions within 72 hours of immunization.

Special consideration and appropriate advice should be sought for the following groups of children:
• Those with a documented history of cerebral damage in the neonatal period
• Those with a personal history of convulsions

- Those whose parents or siblings have a history of idiopathic epilepsy. However, these children may be at risk of developing a similar condition regardless of the vaccine

For all these children the effects of whooping cough disease may be worse than possible risk from the vaccine.

No child should be refused pertussis immunization without appropriate specialist advice.

Poliomyelitis
Neither breastfeeding nor antibiotic therapy are contraindications to receiving polio vaccine.

If the baby vomits within an hour of receiving the vaccine, repeat the dose the following day.

Diphtheria
For primary immunization of those over 10 years, diphtheria vaccine for adults (low dose) should be given.

Tetanus
Reinforcing doses should not be given to anyone known to have received a booster dose within the previous 5−10 years unless there is a high risk of tetanus.

Rubella
All girls should be vaccinated with single antigen rubella vaccine between their 10th and 14th birthdays unless there is documented evidence that they have received MMR vaccine.

Non-pregnant seronegative women of child-bearing age should be vaccinated and advised not to become pregnant within 1 month of vaccination, because of the theoretical risk of harm to the foetus.

Women found to be seronegative on antenatal screening should be vaccinated at delivery.

Haemophilus influenzae type B

This is the most common bacterial cause of meningitis and epiglottitis in children under 5 years. Babies and toddlers are at particular risk. About 1300 children are affected every year, with over 65 deaths. Many children may be left with permanent damage to the central nervous system.

Irritability and occasional slight fever or redness at the site of the injection may occur, but there are no serious reactions documented.

National immunization schedule

The recommended national immunization schedule and intervals are given in Table 3.2.

Passive immunization with human immunoglobulins

Immediate passive immunity lasting a few weeks can be obtained either by injection of human immunoglobulin (HNIG) or specific immunoglobulins. HNIG contains antibody to measles, mumps, varicella, hepatitis A and other viruses which are prevalent in the general population. There are specific immunoglobulins for varicella, tetanus, rabies and hepatitis B.

All immunoglobulins are obtained from the pooled plasma of blood donors or convalescent patients, all of whom are HIV negative.

Prophylaxis for children at special risk should be given as soon as possible after exposure to specific disease, for example measles, chicken pox and hepatitis B. These children may be at risk because of immunosuppression, for example leukaemics; or contact with a disease, for example neonates born 6 days or less after onset of maternal chicken pox; or infants to HBsAg positive mothers.

3.2   Anaphylaxis

This is an allergic reaction which may occur following certain drugs, for example penicillin or ACTH, insect stings or foods.

Table 3.2 Recommended national immunization schedule and intervals

Age	Vaccine	Interval
Primary immunization		
Birth	BCG if appropriate	
2 months	Polio Diphtheria Tetanus Pertussis Hib if available	
3 months	Polio Diphtheria Tetanus Pertussis Hib if available	4 weeks between first and second
4 months	Polio Diphtheria Tetanus Pertussis Hib if available	4 weeks between second and third
12–18 months	Measles/Mumps/ Rubella	3 weeks between live vaccines or different sites simultaneously
Secondary immunization		
4–5 years	Polio Diphtheria Tetanus	
Tertiary immunization		
10–14 years	Rubella (girls only)	
10–14 years	BCG	3 weeks between BCG and rubella
15–18 years	Polio Tetanus	

American and Dutch experiences show that death due to anaphylaxis following immunization, if it has ever occurred, is less than 1 in 30 million doses (Sefi, Macfarlane, 1989).

Signs and symptoms
- Sudden collapse — fall of blood pressure
- Pallor
- Dyspnoea with asthmatic symptoms
- Urticaria
- Occasionally respiratory and cardiac arrest

Treatment
If collapse is profound (i.e. not a simple faint) and recovery does not follow within a few minutes:
- Ask someone to dial 999 and summon medical aid
- Treat for shock, lie the child down and maintain an airway
- Adrenalin 1:1000 should be given i.m., slowly, and at a different injection site from the immunization (Table 3.3)
- Apply CPR as necessary and maintain until emergency services arrive
- If there is no response within 5 minutes, repeat the dose of adrenaline
- Record the reaction and notify the child's GP

Table 3.3 Doses of adrenaline 1:1000

Age	Dose (ml)
< 1 year	0.05
1 year	0.1
2 years	0.2
3—4 years	0.3
5 years	0.4
6—10 years	0.5
11—16	0.7
Adult	1.0

3.3 Allergy and asthma

Allergy

Allergy is a hypersensitive reaction to a foreign protein, when the protein interacts with the antibodies that are produced against it. Breastfeeding, whilst it does not always prevent the development of allergy, is the most satisfactory means of avoiding allergy and should be encouraged, especially in families with a history of atopy, for at least the first 4 months and preferably the first 6 months of life.

General features of allergy
- A family history of allergy
- One child in three is affected
- Delay in exposing to allergens leads to a delay in manifestation but is not preventive
- Most allergic syndromes usually become less intense with age, whilst some may not develop for several years
- Individuals suffering from one allergy are more susceptible to others
- Repeated exposure to a substance often increases the likelihood of an allergy to that substance (e.g. drugs such as penicillin)
- No therapy is curative but merely minimizes exposure or symptoms

Symptoms of allergy are recognized chiefly in the respiratory and gastrointestinal systems and the skin, but may affect any organ system. See Table 3.4 pp. 90—91 for allergens.

Asthma

Asthma is a transient narrowing of the large and small bronchi usually, but not always, accompanied by wheezing and breathlessness. Ten per cent of the population have asthma and it is the most common, treatable chronic medical condition of childhood. However, it is under diagnosed and under treated and is an important cause of school absence and reduced participation in physical education.

Diagnosis

There is usually a positive family history of allergy. Asthma should be suspected in any child with recurrent chestiness or cough. It may only appear in response to exercise, breathing cold air or with infection or other non-allergic exposures. However, it is frequently associated with upper respiratory allergies and eczema. Asthma tends to improve with age.

Evaluation and treatment of children's asthma are important in order to maximize their potential. Chest X-rays are taken to rule out other causes such as chest infection. Peak flow levels are used to measure the severity of the asthma and to evaluate treatment. Skin tests may be useful in order to avoid allergic responses to causes such as pets or house dust.

Treatment is either preventive drug therapy, such as sodium cromoglycate and beclomethasone, or treating attacks with drugs such as salbutamol or terbutaline. These may be administered either orally or in various forms of inhaler. Steroids may be used in severe attacks and very occasionally on a long term basis to prevent attacks.

Technique in administering drugs by inhaler is vital, and attention should be given to their correct use. It is necessary that the child and parents recognize the importance of taking medication properly and regularly, so that the child may lead a normal life.

Hay fever and upper respiratory tract allergy

Twenty per cent of the population suffer from chronic rhinitis at some point during their lives, of which 30% will be due to allergy. Seasonal allergic rhinitis with rhinoconjunctivitis occurs in 5–10% of the population and causes much distress to the sufferer. Treatment is by antihistamine, nasal decongestants and eye drops.

Food intolerance and allergy

Food intolerance and allergy differs from food aversion. Food intolerance produces an abnormal and reproducible unpleasant, or adverse reaction to a specific food or food ingredient, even when that food is disguised. Food allergy produces an abnormal immunological reaction to specific foods. Food aversion incorporates psychological avoidance such as food refusal in toddlers or anorexia nervosa in adolescents.

Food allergy occurs in varying estimates of between 0.3 and 20% of children, with cow's milk intolerance the most common with a prevalence of 0.2–7.5%. The incidence frequently decreases with age (see Table 3.4). Breastfeeding is particularly advocated for infants where there is a strong family history of allergy.

Food allergy may cause anaphylaxis with a type I immune response usually causing an immediate reaction. Skin reactions, such as urticaria or atopic eczema, may occur. Migraine is also recognized as a reaction to some foods. Behavioural disorders may be due to certain foods or artificial colourings and preservatives. Gastrointestinal symptoms include vomiting, diarrhoea, abdominal pain, malabsorption, failure to thrive, enteropathy with small intestinal damage and gastrointestinal blood loss or colitis.

3.4 Breastfeeding

There is no better nutrition for infants than breast milk. Whilst the majority of women (64%) in the UK choose to breastfeed, only 26% of those are still fully breastfeeding at 4 months (Fig. 3.1). The DHSS (1988) recommended that all parents should have the opportunity to discuss breastfeeding with a well informed person during the antenatal period, and that ways should be found both to encourage breastfeeding amongst those sections of the community where it is not popular and to make it more socially acceptable.

For most women it is a pleasant and satisfying experience, but for some it can be a source of frustration and lead to resentment

Table 3.4 Common types of allergic reaction

Age	Allergens	Sex distribution	Common allergic symptoms
Birth–6 months	Primary foods	Male > Female 2:1	Pylorospasm and colic — projectile vomiting Chronic diarrhoea Atopic eczema Persistent nasal congestion with recurrent respiratory infections
6–12 months	Food 66% Environmental inhalants (dust, chemicals, etc) 34%	Male > Female 2:1	Atopic eczema Chronic diarrhoea with or without growth failure Chronic nasal congestion Asthma
1–5 years	Food 25% Environmental inhalants 70% Pollens 5%	Male > Female 2:1	Atopic eczema (spontaneous improvement in 75% by age 3 years) Chronic respiratory infections Chronic nasal congestion without fever Asthma Persistent middle ear fluid

Age	Allergens	Sex ratio	Clinical features
5–12 years	Food 5% Environmental inhalants 25% Pollens 20% Combined inhalants (environmental and pollens) 50%	Male > Female 2:1	Chronic nasal congestion, eustachian tube dysfunction and hearing loss (serous otitis, secretory otitis) School problems (poor attendance, poor attention span) Hay fever (seasonal) Asthma Exercise-induced asthma Urticaria
12–21 years	Food 5% Environmental inhalants and pollens 95%	Male = Female 1:1	Nasal congestion (perennial) Hay fever (seasonal) Exercise-induced asthma Asthma Chronic sinus disease Allergic bronchitis Urticaria

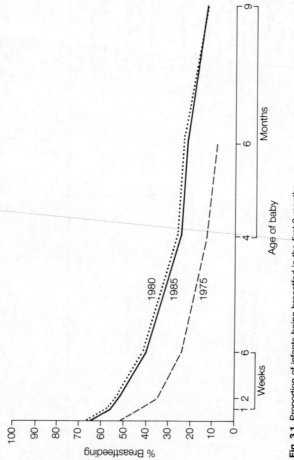

Fig. 3.1 Proportion of infants being breastfed in the first 9 months: England and Wales (OPCS Survey 1975, 1980, 1985).

of the baby. For these women, there should be flexibility with breastfeeding so that they may be encouraged to continue.

The advantages of breastfeeding
- Involution of the uterus
- Decrease in the risk of post partum haemorrhage
- Decrease in the incidence of gastro-enteritis, otitis media, respiratory and some viral infections, milk allergies, asthma, eczema and dental caries.

Factors which help
- A successful first feed — usually within 2 hours of delivery — with adequate support and encouragement from the midwife.
- Correct positioning of the baby. A baby who is properly attached will have a mouth full of breast, including the nipple, much of the areola and the underlying tissue which includes the lactiferous sinuses. The jaw muscles will be seen to be working rhythmically as far back as the ears, the baby will be relaxed, and there should be no pain for the mother.
- The baby should be allowed to determine the frequency and duration of the feeds. The baby should finish the first breast before being offered the second, and the mother be reassured that there will be no imbalance in milk supply, providing she starts with the other breast at the next feed.
- A baby will need to feed at night, and it is advisable for mothers to have their infants near them, either in their beds or a cot nearby.
- Breastfed babies' stools are bright yellow but do not necessarily move at regular intervals. A breastfed baby is never constipated and no intervention is required.
- Hunger and thirst will regulate the minimal extra calorific and fluid requirements of a lactating mother.
- There is no reason to advise a lactating mother to omit any particular food from her diet unless or until the situation dictates otherwise. However, some women with a family history of allergy may benefit from dietary modification such as cow's milk protein,

both during pregnancy and lactation. Medical opinion should be sought.

● Additional fluids for the infant – supplementary or complementary feeds of either water, glucose/dextrose or formula are unnecessary, and have been shown to have no effect in the treatment of physiological jaundice (Nicoll *et al.*, 1982).

● Antenatal preparation of breasts or nipples is of no value. Nipple soreness is not related either to maternal colouring or the skin's toughness. Similarly as the nipple plays no active part in the mechanism of milk release, nipple shape is of no relevance either.

● Adequate personal hygiene is the only postnatal care required, and there is no evidence to show that creams, ointments, etc. have any use in the prevention or treatment of sore nipples.

● Sore nipples can be treated by re-positioning or resting and expressing. Close attention to feeding technique ('re-positioning') is more effective as it causes no interference to the baby's feeding regimen.

● The baby and the baby's father are the greatest sources of encouragement in a mother's decision to breastfeed.

3.5   Bottle feeding

Some mothers will choose to give their babies infant formula from birth, and the majority of babies will be fed infant formula by the age of 4 weeks. It is therefore important that parents receive adequate advice regarding infant formulas and the sterilization of bottles and teats, and are confident about preparing feeds.

Infant formulas are mainly cow's milk based, although some contain other proteins such as soya protein. The cow's milk based formula are either whey based or casein based (Table 3.5). There are no important differences between the two types, and mothers should be encouraged not to change brands or types of formula.

Domestic microwave ovens should not be used for sterilizing bottles or for heating feeds once they are in the bottle. This is

Table 3.5 Cow's milk based infant formulas

Whey based formula	Casein based formula
SMA Gold Cap (Wyeth)	SMA White Cap (Wyeth)
Premium (Cow and Gate)	Plus (Cow and Gate)
Osterfeed (Farley)	Ostermilk Complete Formula
	Ostermilk Two (Farley)
Aptamil (Milupa)	Milumil (Milupa)

because hot fluid at the centre of the bottle may be undetected and scald the infant.

Samples of infant formula must not be distributed to mothers at any time.

Sheep or goats' milk should not be given to infants under 6 months. For older children it should be pasteurized or boiled and vitamin supplements may be necessary.

Follow up milks are expensive and have no advantage over breast milk or infant formula for the first year.

Fully skimmed milk is unsuitable for children under 5 because of its low energy and vitamin A content. Within family meals, for young children who are eating and thriving, semi-skimmed milk may be progressively introduced from the age of 2 years.

Breastfed babies rarely require extra fluids and thirsty babies should be offered cooled, boiled water. A wide variety of infant drinks exist to flavour water, but they all contain sugar and should not be recommended. If this recommendation is ignored, then dilute (1:8) unsweetened fruit juices may be offered from 4 weeks.

All tap water given to babies under 6 months should be boiled. Bottled or softened water should not be used because of the high mineral content. Carbonated drinks are unsuitable for infants.

Soya based milks may be recommended where there is a strong family history of allergy. However, exclusion of cow's milk should be carried out in a controlled manner under the guidance of a GP/paediatrician and dietitian so that the child is not put at risk of lacking calcium and energy.

3.6   Feeding problems in babies

Colic
This may be known as 'evening' or '3 month' colic, as it often occurs during the evening and lasts for about 3 months. However, for some babies it continues for much longer, causing pain to both baby and parents. There are several theories concerning colic, and mothers who are breastfeeding may find dietary restrictions help. This should be done with professional dietetic advice. There are a variety of proprietary remedies available for the treatment of colic, but they do not always achieve relief.

Wind
Wind is a complex subject which in Western society may be a problem. It is more commonly a result of crying rather than the cause of it, and can usually be prevented by more feeding or more attention. In bottle fed babies it may be caused by the hole in the teat being either too large or too small! Whether or not wind is a problem, burping seems to give satisfaction to mother and baby alike.

Posseting and vomiting
Simple regurgitation of a mouthful of food at the end of a feed is called posseting, and should not be confused with vomiting. Babies who feed hurriedly may vomit; this can be avoided by shorter intervals between feeds or more frequent winding. True vomiting with other symptoms often occurs at the onset of infective illness. Projectile vomiting occurs in pyloric stenosis and further advice should be sought.

Constipation
Constipated stools in bottle fed babies are hard and passed with straining and discomfort, sometimes causing a small anal fissure. Constipation may be caused by underfeeding, and regulating the amount of feed will solve the problem. Extra fluids or well-diluted fresh orange juice (1:8) may be the only treatment necessary for

other causes. Very occasionally constipation may be due to a malfunctioning bowel, for example Hirschprung's disease, and further investigation is needed.

Teething
Many teeth appear without any disturbance, but a teething baby may suffer pain. It does not explain every time a baby cries or is unwell, and does not make babies ill. Frequently whilst teething, babies want less milk, and may refuse sieved or lumpy foods.

Crying
Crying is a baby's way of asking for attention. It may be caused by hunger, being too hot or too cold, a wet/dirty nappy or because of boredom or loneliness. Small babies cannot be spoilt and extra cuddling and comforting may help both mother and baby. If a baby cries and shows signs of being unwell, this requires further attention.

Oral thrush
Small white flecks appear on the inside of the cheek or tongue which are difficult to remove. In severe infections the mucosa looks raw, with a glazed red appearance. The angles of the mouth may also become infected. Treatment is with oral nystatin suspension. Oral thrush is a common cause of a baby being reluctant to suck.

3.7 Introduction of solids
Very few infants will require solid foods before the age of 3 months, but the majority should be offered a mixed diet by the age of 6 months. It is inadvisable to introduce solids too early because the infant gut is more vulnerable to infection and allergy, as well as developing a predisposition to obesity from energy-dense foods. The weaning process is a gradual one from the introduction of semi-solid foods, to the introduction to family mealtimes by the age of 1 year.

From 4 months onwards

One or two of the daytime milk feeds can be replaced by other foods. Initially soft purees without lumps, soft, mashed vegetables and fruits are the foods of choice.

Commercial weaning foods have no advantage over foods prepared at home and are considerably more expensive. Home cooked foods should not have any added sugar or salt. Rice should be the first cereal food to be introduced because of the possibility of wheat intolerance. Weaning foods should be fed from a spoon, not added to bottles.

Yoghurt and yoghurt-based desserts should not be given before the age of 6 months, because of the cow's milk content.

From 8 to 10 months

Purees give way to minced foods, finely grated cheese and creamed foods. Egg white should not be given before 8 months because of the risk of intolerance. Eggs should be hard boiled. Crusts of bread, pieces of apple and finger foods — given with supervision because of the risk of choking — will encourage chewing. Natural wholegrain cereals and bread should be encouraged, but bran and fortified foods are unsuitable in the young child because of the risk of trace mineral malabsorption. Nuts should not be introduced to children under 5 years, because of the risk of choking. Drinks can be given from a cup.

By 1 year of age

The child's feeding times should be integrated into family mealtimes. Casseroles of fish and meat may be given and the child be encouraged to feed him or herself with finger foods and to use a spoon (at about 18 months) and cup (at about 12 months).

Between 18 months and 2 years of age the child can seat him or herself at table and from 3 years should be given the opportunity to use a knife and fork.

Children under 5 years of age require approximately 500 ml of milk per day for dietary needs. 180 ml of milk provides the same calcium intake as 30 g of hard cheese or a 150 ml pot of yoghurt. Milk can be incorporated in soups and sauces, such as custard.

3.8   Feeding problems in older children

Other interests may replace the central concern for food at the toddler stage, and it is normal for a child at some time to refuse food. Food refusal is a problem to parents, but not the child, as he/she soon learns how to use it as a powerful weapon. Food should never be forced on reluctant children, as this may cause mealtime rebellion. The following suggestions may be helpful for parents:

- Food should be served in small, attractively presented portions
- Meals should be served at regular intervals; snacks between mealtimes should be either fruit, bread or milk
- Mealtimes should be enjoyable without the distractions of family arguments, television, or the emotional strain of rushed meals
- Children will eat when they are hungry, but quickly learn that food is a convenient weapon with which to manipulate parents for attention. Sufficient attention at other times will help alleviate mealtime rebellion
- New foods and flavours should be introduced gradually. If a food is rejected, allow some time to elapse before reintroducing it
- Children are individuals and have their own likes and dislikes. They will also copy their parents, so the latter should make sure that they pass on the habits which they want their children to follow. For the same reason, the dislikes of other family members should not be discussed in front of children

The daily requirements of healthy children are given in Table 3.6.

3.9   Vitamin and iron supplements

Vitamin supplementation under the DHSS recommendations should be given to all infants from the age of 6 months (or from 1 month in some cases) up to at least 2 years and preferably 5

Table 3.6 Daily requirements of healthy children

Age range	Energy (kcal)	Protein (g)	Vitamin A retinal (µg)	Thiamine (mg)	Nicotinic acid (mg)	Ascorbic acid (Vitamin C) (mg)	Vitamin D (µg)
Infants							
0–6 months	*117	2.2*	450	0.3	5	20	7.5
6–12 months	*108	2.0*	450	0.3	5	20	7.5
Boys							
1–4 years	1200–1600	30–39	300	0.5–0.6	7–9	20	10.0
5–11 years	1740–2280	43–57	300–575	0.7–0.9	10–14	20–25	
12–17 years	2640–2880	66–72	725–750	1.1–1.2	16–19	25–30	
Girls							
1–4 years	1100–1500	27–37	300–	0.4–0.6	7–9	20	10.0
5–11 years	1680–2050	42–51	300–575	0.7–0.8	10–14	20–25	
12–17 years	2150	53	725–750	0.9	16–19	25–30	

* Per kg body weight per day

(Adapted from DHSS 1985 revision, NRC 1980 and WHO 1974)

years. The daily dose of 5 drops will contain approximately: vitamin A — 200 μg; vitamin C — 20 mg; vitamin D — 7 μg.

Sources of vitamins and the dangers of deficiencies are given in Table 3.7.

Foods containing iron should form part of mixed feeding for breastfed babies from 6 months of age, when iron stores become depleted. Most infant formulas are fortified with iron and thus the continued use of formula throughout infancy will ensure adequate iron intake for babies who are no longer breastfed, as well as bottle fed infants.

3.10 Diets of different cultures and beliefs

Some racial groups have cultural or religious dietary restrictions. Ethnic minority groups in the UK frequently follow the diet of their country of origin, but changes may occur owing to the lack of availability of certain foods, or prohibitive cost. Help may be required to advise on suitable alternatives and their preparation, especially during the weaning stages, to ensure an adequate diet and to eliminate any potential nutrient deficiencies.

The commonest cultural and religious diets

1 Jews exclude pork, rabbit, shellfish, etc. Meat must be ritually slaughtered (Kosher). Milk and its products and meat cannot be eaten at the same meal. During Passover, only unleavened bread is allowed.

2 Moslems exclude pork and all forms of carnivorous animals. Meat must be ritually slaughtered (Halal) and alcohol is strictly forbidden.

3 Hindus and Sikhs usually exclude beef and pork. Eggs are frequently excluded, but milk may be allowed. Fasting is a feature, and strict dietary laws apply during special religious festivals.

4 Vegetarianism occurs amongst all peoples regardless of country or creed, and is becoming increasingly popular. Meat is excluded and no fish, flesh or fowl is eaten. Some vegetarians exclude milk and eggs (lacto ova vegetarians), whilst others

Table 3.7 Sources of vitamins and dangers of deficiencies

Vitamin	Chemical product	Natural sources	Clinical deficiency
A	Retinol	Fish-liver oils, carrots and carotene-containing vegetables; sheep and ox liver; margarine; dairy produce	Abnormalities of skin and mucous membrane Night blindness Defective growth Infection
B complex. In addition to thiamine (B_1), riboflavine and nicotinic acid, the B complex contains folic acid, pantothenic acid, pyridoxine, cobalamin, biotin, etc	Thiamine (B_1)	Yeast, Marmite, wheat and rice germ, egg yolk, liver, roe, peas and beans, bread	Beri-beri Wernicke's encephalopathy Korsakoff's syndrome
	Riboflavine (B_2)	Yeast, milk, egg white, liver, roe, leaf vegetables	Angular stomatitis Seborrhoeic dermatitis Corneal vascularization
	Nicotinic acid	Yeast, meat, peanuts, unpolished rice, bread	Pellagra Dementia Dermatitis

C	Ascorbic acid	Orange, lemon, blackcurrant, tomato juice; swedes, spinach, watercress, cabbage; rose-hips.	Scurvy
D	Calciferol (D_2)	Irradiation of pro-vitamin on or in skin by sunlight, fish-liver oils, dairy produce	Rickets Tetany
E	Alpha, beta and gamma tocopherol	Wheatgerm, green leaves	Infertility Abortion (miscarriage)
K	Phylloquinone	Alfalfa, spinach, cauliflower, cabbage, soya bean, etc. (Possibly synthesized in gut by bacterial action)	Hypoprothrombinaemia Haemorrhagic disease of newborn
P	Citrin	Blackcurrant, grape, lemon, orange juice, rosehips	Increased capillary permeability

exclude eggs but not milk (ova vegetarians), and some milk but not eggs (lacto vegetarians).

5 Vegans exclude all animal products, i.e. meat, dairy products, eggs and honey. Protein is obtained from pulses and cereal combinations.

Well-informed vegetarians and vegans give their children satisfactory diets, but parents with a poor knowledge of these diets may need advice at the weaning and toddler stages, and supplementation of iron and vitamin B_{12} may be necessary.

3.11 Special therapeutic diets

Diets adopted for medical or metabolic disorders in conditions such as phenylketonuria, coeliac disease and diabetes require paediatric dietetic advice.

Phenylketonuria is an inborn error of amino acid metabolism, and dietary restriction of phenylalanine is essential to prevent severe mental deficiency. Conversely phenylalanine deficiency can lead to failure to thrive, vomiting, diarrhoea, eczema and brain damage, and it is important that close medical and dietetic supervision ensure correct dietary modification.

Coeliac disease is a disorder of absorption caused by the damaging effects of dietary gluten on the bowel mucosa. Its effect is growth failure, wasting, abdominal distension, steatorrhoea and anaemia. Treatment is with a gluten free diet, i.e. nothing containing wheat or rye flour.

Diabetes mellitus is caused by diminished insulin secretion or utilization which can result in hyperglycaemia, glycosuria, ketosis and in untreated cases, coma and death. Treatment is with insulin and dietary modification to ensure normal growth and utilization of all insulin given.

3.12 Dental care

During pregnancy

From about the eighth week of pregnancy, the baby's first teeth are beginning to form. At birth all the deciduous (milk) teeth are present in the jaws as well as some of the permanent teeth. During pregnancy a normal balanced diet is sufficient to ensure normal formation of the baby's teeth. The mother should visit the dentist at least twice during pregnancy.

Ages of eruption

During infancy
Twenty deciduous teeth begin to erupt at about 5—7 months and tooth eruption continues until about 30—36 months (Fig. 3.2(a)). Toothbrushing, with a soft baby brush at first, should begin as soon as teeth appear. The toothpaste can be any standard proprietary brand containing fluoride and from 6 months fluoride supplements can be given (see fluoride advice below).

First visit to the dentist
Small children should visit the dentist, preferably with the parents, for regular check-ups from 2 to 3 years of age onwards. The deciduous teeth are just as important as the permanent teeth. Early treatment, if necessary, is much easier and better than extraction, but when pain is experienced it is often too late.

The second or permanent teeth
These begin to erupt at 6 years or just before, and the first to appear is a large molar just behind the baby molars. Then at about 7 years the permanent incisor teeth begin to displace the baby incisors, which are shed; this process of replacement goes on until at least 11 years of age (Fig. 3.2(b)).

Fluoride supplements
Fluoridation of water and the use of fluoride toothpaste has dramatically decreased the incidence of dental caries. The daily fluoride intake approved by the Dental Health Committee of the British Dental Association is:

Deciduous teeth

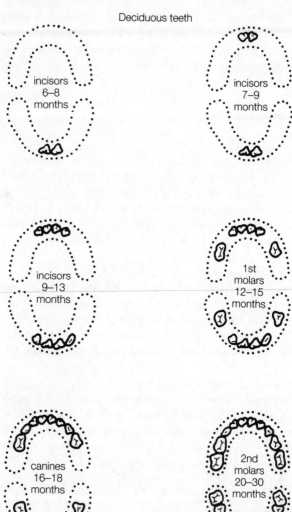

(a)

Permanent teeth

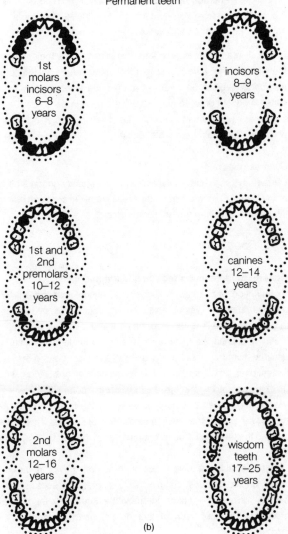

Fig. 3.2 Growth of teeth at different ages.

0.25 mg fluoride from 2 weeks to 2 years	where the fluoride
0.5 mg fluoride from 2 to 4 years	level of water is
1 mg fluoride from 4 to 16 years	below 0.3 ppm

Artificially fed infants in fluoridated areas can satisfy their requirements from the water used to reconstitute feeds. Health professionals need to be aware of the fluoride levels in their local water supply in order to give accurate advice to parents.

Fluoride supplementation may be given by tablet or drops, which are available from the chemist.

Sources of advice
Dental advice is readily available from community dental staff in many Health Centres or from the Area Dental Officer, from whom information and literature is also available.

3.13 Foot care

General guidelines on foot inspection and care
Examination of the baby's feet should ensure that there is no obvious deformity (valgus ankles, metatarsus varus, pes cavus, talipes, etc.) and that each foot has a full range of movement.

When a child starts to walk, the feet and legs sometimes assume slightly 'abnormal postures' such as bowing at the knees, or external rotation of the feet. As walking ability increases up to the age of 2 years, these almost always correct themselves. At this stage parents sometimes think that the fatty tissue under the medial arch of the foot is an indication of flat feet. This is not so, and the fat disappears as the muscles of the feet develop with use.

Infants should not have shoes or socks until they start walking out of doors. Bootees, sleeping suits, and stretch suits, should always have ample space for movement to allow for normal growth of the feet. Normal feet do not need 'supporting' or 'bracing'.

Outdoor walking needs appropriate footwear, and emphasis should be placed on having shoes expertly fitted and frequently replaced to allow for growth. The structure of the child's foot is very pliable and serious malformation can result from poorly fitting footwear. It is usually painless and therefore often unnoticed.

The feet of children from 2 years onwards should be examined for straightness of the inner and outer foot borders from heel to the 1st and 5th toes. All toes should point straight ahead. Toe deviation or twisting may lead to serious forefoot problems in later life.

The skin of children's feet tends to be moist and this can lead to maceration, particularly between the toes. Advice about hygiene is therefore important. Should there be cause for concern with signs of inflammation, itching interdigitally, signs of verrucae, signs of athlete's foot or other specific skin lesions, further advice should be sought from a GP or chiropodist.

Common problems of the feet and legs

Flat feet in children may often cause concern to the parents, but the condition rarely continues into adulthood. As long as the child's feet are symmetrical, asymptomatic, adopt a plantigrade position on weightbearing and have normal joint, muscle and nerve function, they should be regarded as normal. Very occasionally minor shoe modification is needed. In all cases the parents should be warned that children with flat feet are hard on footwear.

Knock knees, if they are symmetrical with not more than 10 cm between the medial malleoli when the knees are together, can be regarded as within normal limits. The condition usually arises when the child begins to walk, and as long as this gap is not exceeded it does not need treatment.

Bow legs are often present at birth but may not be noticed till later. The bowing is almost always symmetrical and usually disappears within 4 years, with no treatment needed.

Curly toes are usually a minor variation in the outer toes. Some seem to grow straight later. They should be left alone unless further symptoms occur.

In-toeing, or 'pigeon-toeing', may be due to anteversion of the femoral head or due to 'hooking' of the forefoot. If there is anteversion of the femoral head when the child begins to walk there will be 'squinting' of the patellae and internal rotation of the leg will be increased at the expense of external rotation. As the child grows the condition tends to improve and only very rarely is anything further than an explanation and reassurance needed. In 'hooking' of the forefoot the rest of the foot is normal, and the hooking of the forefoot can usually be corrected by gentle pressure. The outlook is good with spontaneous correction usually occurring by the age of 3 years. Hooked forefeet are best managed by an orthopaedic surgeon.

Limitation of abduction of legs when in flexion should always give rise to the suspicion of hip dislocation with dysplasia until proved otherwise. However, loss of abduction in flexion may also be associated with the 'moulded baby syndrome' when there is plagiocephaly of the head, or mild torticollis and scoliosis. In such cases an X-ray of the hips shows normal results. However, all such children should be referred to an orthopaedic surgeon for supervision.

If a malformation is suspected or if a child is complaining of foot pain, he or she should be referred as soon as possible to a paediatrician, orthopaedic surgeon or chiropodist, depending on the nature of the problem.

Further reading and references

DOH (1990) *Immunisation against Infectious Disease*, HMSO, London
DHSS (1988) *Present Day Practice in Infant Feeding*, Third Report, HMSO, London
Francis D. (1986) *Nutrition for Children*, Blackwell Scientific Publications Ltds, Oxford

Gold M., Zimmerman B. *et al.* (1986) *Allergies and Children*, Kids Can Press, Toronto

Nicoll A. *et al.* (1982) Supplementary feeding and jaundice in newborns, *Acta Paediatr Scand,* **71**, 759−61

Oxfordshire Health Authority (1988) *Food and Health Policy for the Under 5s*, Dept. of Nutrition and Dietetics, Oxford

RCM (1988) *Successful Breastfeeding*, Holywell Press, Oxford

Sefi S., Macfarlane A. (1989) *Immunizing Children*, Oxford Medical Publications, Oxford

Warner J., Goldsworthy S. *Childhood Asthma*, Paediatrics Dept., Brompton Hospital, London

World Health Organization (1985) *Targets for Health For All*, Copenhagen

4   Disability and handicap in the community

Early identification of handicap in a child is important to prevent the handicap becoming more serious and to prevent or treat secondary handicaps (such as visual abnormalities in children with cerebral palsy).

The Children Act 1989 makes provision for 'children in need' and specifically includes within that group children with disabilities. It behoves local authorities to take reasonable steps to identify and maintain a register of disabled children, as well as publicizing and providing services for them.

Most handicapped children are cared for at home rather than in institutions, but a continual shortage of services and facilities often makes families feel they have not received sufficient help or information. All families with a handicapped member will be disadvantaged and deprived in some way, regardless of what provision is made for them. For many there may be financial hardship as well as emotional difficulties and lack of support.

Siblings of handicapped children may feel resentment of the extra care and attention given to the handicapped child, and it is important in assessment that the needs of brothers and sisters be examined and provision for them be considered as well.

Parental reaction to the news of a disability or handicap is initially acute shock and grief. As this subsides anger and denial manifest themselves, with parents often becoming overwhelmed with caring for the child and sometimes seeking miracle or magical cures. The enormity of the situation can put a great strain on relationships. Help and support are vital in promoting healthy adaptation by mobilization of resources both within the family and community.

4.1   Physical handicap

Physical handicap may be defined as any loss of anatomical structure or function. It may be classified according to aetiology or the pattern of the motor disability. Whilst severe handicaps will require a greater and more continuous input from a wide range of professional services, the lesser handicaps will nevertheless require support and care for the child and the family.

Physical handicap may result in temporary loss of function, for example an orthopaedic abnormality which may be corrected by surgery, or a permanent loss of function of varying severity. The most common examples of physical handicap are cerebral palsy, spina bifida and muscular dystrophy, which result in a multiplicity of associated handicaps.

4.2 Mental handicap

The mentally handicapped child has reduced intellectual capacity to the point of impaired learning ability and social functioning. The handicap may be discovered either at birth, for example Down's syndrome, or during the first year or so of life, by the parents suspecting that something is wrong.

If the diagnosis is made at birth, it is important that the parents be informed as soon as possible. Counselling and support for all family members should be available.

4.3 District handicap and assessment teams

These may be either a single organization, or separate teams with close links. The initial aim is to provide a multidisciplinary approach in the assessment of children with handicaps. Any of the following professionals may be involved; community and/or hospital paediatricians, paediatric neurologist, orthopaedic surgeon, audiologist, ophthalmologist, psychiatrist, psychologist, geneticist, physiotherapist, occupational therapist, educational psychologist, speech therapist, teachers, specialist nurses, health visitors and social workers.

The team approach is based on optimizing the child's potential by planning a co-ordinated schedule of treatment and follow up care in conjunction with the parents and providing continuing advice and support to parents and families. It is important that all members of the family are considered within the care framework, with particular attention to siblings.

4.4   Benefits for children with disabilities

A handicapped child may be entitled to some or all of the allowances below. These benefits are covered by 'residency' rules, and local social security offices should be contacted for more information and details.

Attendance Allowance (AA)

This is payable for any child under 16 years of age, who requires attention or supervision 'substantially in excess of that normally required by a child of the same age and sex'. It is a tax-free, non-means tested benefit, and is payable to anyone satisfying attendance conditions for at least 6 months. It is payable at two rates; the higher rate is for those who satisfy both the day and night attendance conditions. Otherwise the lower rate is payable.

Mobility Allowance (MA)

This is payable for children over the age of 5 with a physical disability which results in their being 'unable or virtually unable to walk'. It is a tax-free, non-means tested benefit.

Disability Allowance (DA)

This will replace AA and MA from 1992. It will involve one application form and one assessment procedure, but will consist of two components — a care component paid at three different levels, and a mobility component paid at two levels. There will be a 3 month qualifying period.

Invalid Care Allowance (ICA)

This is a taxable benefit paid to persons of working age caring for anyone with a severe disability who receives attendance allowance and requires 'regular and substantial care' (i.e. 35 hours a week or more), when the carer is not 'gainfully' employed (i.e. not earning more than a set amount, as defined by the Department of Social Security).

Disabled Child Premium (DCP)
This is a component part of Income Support, and is payable for any child in a low-income family who receives either AA or MA, or is blind or treated as blind.

Additional payments/benefits

Family Fund
The Family Fund (see section 4.6 for address) was set up to help families with severely handicapped children under 16 with needs which could not be met by existing services. It does not replace statutory provisions made through government, the health services and the local authorities. The fund has to take into account the social and economic circumstances of families, but no means test of income or expenditure is applied.

Independent Living Fund
The Independent Living Fund (see section 4.6 for address) is a charitable trust set up to help severely disabled people with the costs involved in living independently in the community. There are no age limits for those people who may obtain help from the fund.

Free milk
Handicapped children who do not attend school can receive free milk.

Transport and fares
Transport can often be a great difficulty for families with handicapped children. Orange 'disabled' badges confer special parking facilities for cars with passengers who are blind or who have severe walking difficulties. Application is made via local social services departments. Help may also be available for fares to and from hospital for families on low incomes.

Motability

This is a voluntary scheme backed by the DSS (see section 4.6 for address) whereby carers of children receiving MA may be entitled to lease hire a car from Motability.

House adaptation and equipment

The local authority, under the 1970 Chronically Sick and Disabled Persons Act, and the 1986 Disabled Persons (SCR) Act, is responsible for providing people with disabilities with information about the local services which are available. It also has powers to pay for all or part of the cost of adapting a house for a handicapped child or adult, for example by ramps, alterations to baths, lavatories, etc. Application should be made to the social services department.

Special equipment and furniture is often available on loan from occupational therapy departments, which are funded by the health authority and social services departments. Nursing and mobility equipment is the responsibility of health authorities and most other equipment necessary for daily living is the responsibility of social services.

The Disabled Living Foundation (see section 4.6 for address) publishes three lists of equipment available for the general needs, mobility needs and furniture needs of children with handicaps. Similarly there is an illustrated book on equipment available for Disabled Children from Mary Marlborough Lodge, Oxford (see section 4.6 for address).

The Disability Alliance (see section 4.6 for address) is a national organization for people with disabilities. It produces a useful guide, *Disability Rights Handbook*, which is updated annually, as well as offering specialist training courses.

DIAL, the Disability Information Advice Line, offers information about local services in many areas. Check the local telephone directory for details.

4.5   Self help groups

Self help groups are designed to provide information and guidance for people with a common problem, condition, experience or situation. The decrease over the last 30 years of communicable and preventable illness, has shifted the emphasis to chronic illness and disability. Patients have become more informed and active partners in their own care, and the flexibility and capacity for innovation which self help groups enjoy have helped improve the quality of life of both sufferers and their families as well as helping to prevent isolation and lessen some of the stigma of disability.

Self help groups have a dual role in providing information for health care professionals as well as individuals and their families.

4.6 Where to go for help and advice — helping agencies and their addresses

Whilst every care has been taken to ensure that these addresses are correct, changes do take place from time to time.

Action for the care of families whose children have life-threatening and terminal conditions (ACT), Institute of Child Health, Royal Hospital for Sick Children, Bristol BS2 8BJ (Tel: 0272 221556/250652)

Action Research for the Crippled Child, Vincent House, North Parade, Horsham, West Sussex RH12 2DA (Tel: 0403 64101)

Advisory Centre for Education, 18 Victoria Park Square, London E2 9PB (Tel: 081 980 4596)

Anorexic Family Aid and National Information Centre, Sackville Place, 44 – 48 Magdalen Street, Norwich NR3 1JE (Tel: 0603 621414)

Arthritis and Rheumatism Council for Research, 41 Eagle Street, London WC1 4AR (Tel: 071 405 8572)

Association for the Education and Welfare of the Visually Handicapped, (Mrs S Clamp), St Vincents School for the Blind, Yew Tree Lane, W. Derby, Liverpool, Lancs (Tel: 051 228 9968)

Association for Improvements in Maternity Services (AIMS), 163 Liverpool Road, London N1 0RF (Tel: 071 278 5628)

Association for all Speech Impaired Children, 347 Central Markets, Smithfield, London EC1 9NH (Tel: 071 236 6478)

Association for Spina Bifida and Hydrocephalus, 22 Upper Woburn Place, London WC1 0EP (Tel: 071 388 1382)

Asthma Research Council, 300 Upper Street, London N1 2XX (Tel: 071 226 2260)

Baby Life Support System, 44/5 Museum Street, London WC1A 1LY (Tel: 071 831 9393)

Birthright, 27 Sussex Place, Regents Park, London NW1 5SP (Tel: 071 723 9296/ 262 5337)

British Diabetic Association, 10 Queen Anne Street, London W1M 0BD (Tel: 071 323 1531)

British Epilepsy Association, Anstey House, 40 Hanover Square, Leeds LS3 1BE (Tel: 0532 439393)

British Institute of Mental Handicap, Wolverhampton Road, Kidderminster DY10 3PP (Tel: 0562 850251)

British Migraine Association, 178A High Road, Byfleet, Weybridge KT14 7ED (Tel: 09323 52468)

British Paediatric Association, 5 St Andrews Place, London NW1 4LB (Tel: 071 486 6151)

British Pregnancy Advisory Service (BPAS), Austy Manor, Wootton Wawen, Solihull, West Midlands B95 6BX (Tel: 05642 3225)

British Red Cross Society, 9 Grosvenor Crescent, London SW1X 7EJ (Tel: 071 235 5454)

Brook Advisory Centre, 153 East Street, London SE17 2SD (Tel: 071 708 1390)

Cancer and Leukaemia in Childhood Trust, 11/12 Freemantle Square, Cotham, Bristol BS6 5TL (Tel: 0272 48844)

Child Accident Prevention Trust, 75 Portland Place, London W1 (Tel: 071 636 2545)

Child Assault Prevention Programme, 30 Windsor Court, London W2 (Tel: 071 229 7722)

Child Growth Foundation, 2 Mayfield Avenue, Chiswick, London W4 1PW (Tel: 081 994 7625)

Child Poverty Action Group, 1–5 Bath Street, London EC1 9PY (Tel: 071 253 3406)

Cleft Lip and Palate Association, 1 Eastwood Gardens, Kenton, Newcastle upon Tyne, Tyne and Wear NE3 3DQ (Tel: 091 285 9396)

Coeliac Society of the United Kingdom, PO Box 220, High Wycombe, Bucks HP11 2HY (Tel: 0494 37278)

Compassionate Friends, 6 Denmark Street, Bristol BS1 5DQ (Tel: 0272 292778)

Contact a Family, 16 Strutton Ground, London SW1P 2HP (Tel: 071 222 2695)

Cystic Fibrosis Research Trust, Alexandra House, 5 Blyth Road, Bromley, Kent BR1 3RS (Tel: 081 464 7211)

Disabled Living Foundation, 380–384 Harrow Road, London W9 2HU (Tel: 071 289 6111)

Disability Alliance ERA, 25 Denmark Street, London WC2 8NJ Tel: 071 240 0806

Divorce Conciliation and Advisory Services, 38 Ebury Street, London SW1 0LV (Tel: 071 730 2422)

Down's Syndrome Association, 12–13 Clapham Common, Southside, London SW4 7AA (Tel: 071 720 0008)

Eneuresis Resource and Information Centre (ERIC), 65 St Michael's Hill, Bristol, BS2 8DZ (Tel: 0272 264920)

Family Fund, PO Box 50, York YO1 1UY (Tel: 0904 621115)

Family Planning Association, 27–35 Mortimer Street, London W1N 7RJ (Tel: 071 636 7866)

Foundation for the Study of Infant Deaths, 15 Belgrave Square, London SW1X 8PS (Tel: 071 235 1721/0965)

Gingerbread, 35 Wellington Street, London WC2E 7BN (Tel: 071 240 0953)

Haemophilia Society, 123 Westminster Bridge Road, London SE1 7HR (Tel: 071 928 2020)

Health Education Authority, 78 New Oxford Street, London WC1A 1AH (Tel: 071 631 0930)

Hyperactive Children's Support Group, 71 Whyke Lane, Chichester, Sussex (Tel: 0903 725182)

Independent Living Fund, PO Box 183, Nottingham NG8 3RD

Invalid Children's Aid Nationwide (ICAN), Allen Graham House, 198 City Road, London EC1V 2PH (Tel: 071 608 2462)

Kith and Kids, Coram Fields, London WC1 (Tel: 0920 870741)

La Leche League (Great Britain), BM 3424, London WC1 6XX (Tel: 071 242 1278 (any time), 071 404 5011 (office hours)

Mary Marlborough Lodge, Nuffield Orthopaedic Centre, Headington, Oxford OX3 7LD (Tel: 0865 750103)

Maternity Alliance, 59/61 Camden High Street, London NW1 7JL (Tel: 071 388 6337)

MENCAP, 123 Golden Lane, London EC1Y 0RT (Tel: 071 253 9433)

Meet a Mum Association, 3 Woodside Avenue, South Norwood, London SE25 5DW (Tel: 081 654 3137)

Motability, Boundary House, 91–93 Charterhouse Street, London EC1M 6BT

Muscular Dystrophy Group of Great Britain and Northern Ireland, Nattrass House, 35 Macauley Road, London SW4 0QP (Tel: 071 720 8055)

National Association for Gifted Children, 1 South Audley Street, London W1Y 5DQ (Tel: 071 499 1188)

National Association for Maternal and Child Welfare, 1 South Audley Street, London W1Y 6JS (Tel: 071 491 1315)

National Association for the Welfare of Children in Hospital (NAWCH), Argyle House, 29–31 Euston Road, London NW1 2SD (Tel: 071 833 2041)

National Autistic Society, 276 Willesden Lane, London NW2 5RB (Tel: 081 451 3844)

National Childbirth Trust, 9 Queensborough Terrace, London W2 3TB (Tel: 071 229 9319)

National Childminders Association, 8 Masons Hill, Bromley BR2 9EY (Tel: 081 464 6164)

National Children's Bureau, 8 Wakeley Street, London EC1V 7QE (Tel: 071 278 9441)

National Council for One Parent Families, 255 Kentish Town Road, London NW5 2LX (Tel: 071 267 1361)

National Council for Special Education, 1 Wood Street, Stratford upon Avon CV37 6JE (Tel: 0789 205332)

National Council for Voluntary Organisations, 26 Bedford Square, London WC1B 2HU (Tel: 071 636 4066)

National Deaf Children's Society, 45 Hereford Road, London W2 5AH (Tel: 071 229 9272/4)

National Eczema Society, Tavistock House North, Tavistock Square, London WC1H 9SR (Tel: 071 388 4097)

National Society for Epilepsy, Chalfont Centre for Epilepsy, Chalfont St Peter, Bucks SL9 0RJ (Tel: 02407 3991)

National Society for the Prevention of Cruelty to Children, 67 Saffron Hill, London ECIN 8RS (Tel: 071 242 1626) (see also local directories)

National Stepfamily Association, 72 Willesden Lane, London NW6 7TA (Tel: 071 372 0844 (Office) 071 372 0846 (Counselling Service)

National Toy Libraries Association, 68 Churchway, London NW1 1LT (Tel: 071 387 9592)

Newpin (New Parent Infant Network), Sutherland House, Sutherland Square, Walworth, London SE17 3EE (Tel: 071 703 5271)

Parents Anonymous Lifeline, Manor Gardens Centre, Manor Gardens, London N7 (Tel: 071 263 8918)

Patients Association, Room 33, 18 Charing Cross Road, London WC2H 0HR (Tel: 071 240 0671)

Pre-School Playgroups Association, 61–63 Kings Cross Road, London WC1X 9LL (Tel: 071 833 8991)

Relate — National Marriage Guidance Council, Herbert Gray College, Little Church Street, Rugby CV21 3AP (Tel: 0788 73241/60811)

Royal National Institute for the Blind, 224 Great Portland Street, London W1N 6AA (Tel: 071 388 1266)

Royal National Institute for the Deaf, 105 Gower Street, London WC1 6AH (Tel: 071 387 8033)

Royal Society for the Prevention of Accidents, Cannon House, The Priory, Queensway, Birmingham B4 6BS (Tel: 021 200 2461)

Stillbirth and Neonatal Death Society (SANDS), 28 Portland Place, London W1N 4DE (Tel: 071 436 5881)

Sense — The National Deaf–Blind and Rubella Association, 311 Gray's Inn Road, London WC1X 8PT (Tel: 071 278 1005/1000)

Sickle Cell Society, Green Lodge, Barretts Green Road, London NW10 7AP (Tel: 081 961 7795/8346)

Spastics Society, 12 Park Crescent, London W1N 4EQ (Tel: 071 636 5020)

Spinal Injuries Association, 76 St James's Lane, London N10 3DF (Tel: 081 444 2121)

Terence Higgins Trust Ltd, BM AIDS, London WC1N 3XX (Tel: 071 833 2971 (Helpline))

Twins and Multiple Births Association, 20 Redcar Close, Lillington, Leamington Spa, CV32 7SU (Tel: 0926 22688)

Further reading and references

Knights S., Gann R. (1988) *The Self Help Guide*, Chapman and Hall Ltd., London

Lakhani B., Read J., Wood P. (1989) *National Welfare Rights Handbook*, Child Poverty Action Group, London

Polnay L. (1988) *Manual of Community Paediatrics*, Churchill Livingstone, Edinburgh

Robertson S. (1989) *The Disability Rights Handbook*, The Disability Alliance ERA, London

Rowland M., Kennedy C., McMullen J. (1989) *Rights Guide to Non-Means Tested Benefits*, Child Poverty Action Group, London

The Chronically Sick and Disabled Persons Act (1970) HMSO, London

The Disabled Persons Act (SCR) (1986) HMSO, London

Wilson J. (1986) *Self Help Groups*, Longman, Harlow

5 Diseases and other problems

5.1   Care of the sick child

Parents are generally very good at telling whether their children are ill or not, but sometimes important signs may get missed. Part of health education in the home, surgery and child health clinic should be to help the parents recognize when their child is sick. The following symptoms indicate that urgent referral to a doctor is necessary:

- A fit or convulsion or turning blue
- A hoarse croupy cough
- Quick difficult grunting breathing
- Unusual or prolonged crying or other signs that the baby is in severe pain
- Exceptionally hard to wake or remains very drowsy

Two or more of the following symptoms in combination for more than a day should indicate the need for referral to a doctor:

- Snuffles
- Cough
- Irritability
- Vomiting
- Diarrhoea
- Drowsiness
- Rash
- Change of cry
- Fever

The following are signs that the baby or child is not getting enough fluid and will need referral to a doctor:

- Dry mouth
- Sunken fontanelle in babies aged less than 12 months
- Poor urine output, demonstrated by fewer wet nappies (wet nappies may be caused by watery diarrhoea, however)
- Sunken eyes with dark rings around them
- Irritability or drowsiness, lax or doughy skin, especially over the abdomen

Parents should be told how to treat a fever in their child, and also something about febrile convulsions. Instructions to parents on both of these are outlined below.

Treatment of fever

Always remember that a fever is one of the signs that a child is ill. Parents should consult their general practitioner if the child appears unusually ill, or if the fever persists or is unusually high. The following measures will help to lower the child's temperature.

Skin exposure   children lose heat through the skin. If they feel hot, take off most of their clothes. Do not wrap them up because this will raise their temperature.

Fluids   give plenty of fluids. Frequently a child with a fever does not feel hungry, but plenty of fluids will prevent dehydration, may reduce the temperature and will make the child more comfortable.

Aspirin is no longer recommended in the treatment of fever in children under the age of 12 years, because of the association with Reye's syndrome.

Paracetamol, (Panadol, Disprol, Calpol) will lower a child's temperature. A little fever is not dangerous and drug treatment is not always necessary. If the child's temperature is unusually high the following doses may be given: 3 months to 1 year: 60–120 mg; 1 to 2 years: 120–250 mg. This dose may be repeated every 6 hours, but should not be continued as frequently as this for more than 24 hours.

Sponging   if the parent or carer is unable to control the fever with these methods, sponge the child with *lukewarm* water. Do not use cold water as this takes the blood away from the skin and delays cooling. Sponge no more frequently than two hourly and for no longer than half an hour at a time.

Treatment of febrile convulsions

Febrile convulsions are fits which often occur in children up to the age of about 4 years, when their temperature rises rapidly.

If the child has a fit lie him/her on the right side on the bed or on the floor with the face turned toward the floor so that any vomit in the throat will drain out. *Do not attempt to force anything between the teeth or gums*.

If the fit does not stop within 5 minutes contact the GP or take the child to a hospital casualty department.

Vomiting and diarrhoea

There are numerous causes of vomiting in children, and in many cases these will be obvious. The most common causes are listed in Tables 5.1 and 5.2, along with some of their specific features and their management.

The usual cause for concern both with vomiting and diarrhoea is dehydration, the signs of which are dealt with at the beginning of this section (p. 126).

The initial treatment of vomiting or diarrhoea is the attempt to ensure that the child does not lose more fluid than he or she receives. When a child is vomiting, small amounts of fluid should be given frequently by mouth, made up of 1 level teaspoon of sugar/glucose dissolved in 120 ml water. (Unless salt can be rigorously controlled it is best left out.) Approximately 180 ml for each kg of the child's body weight can be given every 24 hours. In older children, Coca-Cola, apple juice or fizzy drinks, with the fizz taken out by stirring, can be used instead.

The commoner causes of diarrhoea are listed on pp. 132–133.

5.2 Infections

Notifiable diseases

All cases of the following infectious diseases should be notified to the relevant doctor at the District Headquarters.

Acute meningitis	*Dysentery*
Anthrax	*Encephalitis*
Cholera	*Food poisoning*
Diphtheria	*Hepatitis A*

Hepatitis B	*Poliomyelitis*
Lassa fever	*Rabies*
Leptospirosis	*Relapsing fever*
Leprosy	*Scarlet fever*
Malaria	*Tetanus*
Marburg disease	*Tuberculosis*
Measles	*Typhoid and paratyphoid*
Meningococcal disease	*Typhus*
Mumps	*Viral haemorrhagic fevers*
Ophthalmia neonatorum	*Whooping cough*
Plague	*Yellow fever*

The incubation and isolation periods of some infectious diseases are given in Table 5.3.

Diseases and infestations that can be carried by household pets are given in Table 5.4.

Tonsillitis and pharyngitis

Throat infections are common in young children and may be caused by Group A streptococci, viruses and many other agents both infectious and non-infectious. The usual treatment is antibiotic therapy, either penicillin or erythromycin in the case of penicillin allergy. However, a positive throat culture should precede the decision to use antibiotic therapy.

Throat culture should be done when the patient has one or more of the following symptoms:

• Fever above 39°C
• Pharyngeal inflammation and exudate
• Petechiae (small haemorrhages) on the soft palate
• Enlarged, tender anterior cervical lymph nodes
• Fine red rash, generalized but sparing the perioral area and accentuated in flexures

Most children with frequent sore throats grow out of them, and tonsillectomy does little to alleviate the problem.

Table 5.1 Causes, characteristics and treatment of vomiting

Causes	Age	Appears ill?	Relation to intake	Fever	Diarrhoea	Management
Physiological ('spitting up')	Infancy	No	Varies	No	No	None
Feeding faults: over-feeding	Infancy	No	Immediate	No	Occasional	Formula management
Poor feeding technique	Infancy	No	Immediate	No	Rare	Instruct mother
Obstruction of GI tract:						
Appendicitis or Meckel's diverticulitum	All ages	Moderately	None	Yes	Occasional	Surgery
Ileus with peritonitis	All ages	Severely	None	Yes	Yes	Chemotherapy and/or surgery
Congenital anomalies	Infancy	No	Varies	No	None	Surgery
Pyloric stenosis	2–8 weeks	No	Varies	No	No	Surgery
Acute infectious diseases: almost any disease with fever at onset. Also pertussis	Under 10 years	Moderately to severely	Immediate	Yes	Occasional in younger ages	Treat specific disease. Nothing by mouth, then liquid diet and finally soft diet
Epidemic vomiting (viral)	All ages	Mild	Varies	Yes	Occasional	Restrict intake. Liquid diet, then soft
Specific enteric infection: epidemic vomiting and diarrhoea, salmonellae or shigellae	All ages	Moderately	Immediate	Usual	Usual	Nothing by mouth, then liquid, then soft diet. Chemotherapy in salmonellae and shigellae
Central nervous system:						
Expansile lesions tumours, haematoma, or oedema	All ages	Moderately	None	No	None	Surgery and parenteral fluids

Acute meningitis	All ages	Severely	None	Yes	None	Treat specific disease Parenteral fluids
Motion sickness	All ages	Mildly	Immediate	No	Occasional in younger ages	Medication
Toxic poisoning	All ages	Moderately	None	No	Occasional	
Food poisoning	All ages	Moderately	Within 6 hours	No	Occasional	Gastric lavage, sedation, parenteral fluids; later liquid diet
Diabetic acidosis	All ages	Severely	None	No	None	Treat diabetes
Psychogenic or emotional: Rumination	Infancy	No	30 min later	No	None	Thicken formula with thickening agent. Sedation
'Cyclic vomiting'	Over 2 years	Occasionally	Immediate and late	Occ.	None	Parenteral fluids, sedation; later soft diet
Simple excitement	All ages	No	Immediate and late	No	None	Sedation and soft diet
Cardiac disease: may be congestive failure or digitalis intoxication	All ages	Perhaps severely	None	No	Rare	Digitalis in failure or stop digitalis if intoxication. Sedation and soft diet
Cardiospasm and oesophageal stricture	All ages	No	Immediate	No	None	Parenteral fluids, sedation; later, liquid diet and soft diet. Dilatation procedures
Achalasia	Infancy	No	Immediate	No	No	Put in upright position after feeding

Table 5.2 Causes, characteristics and treatment of diarrhoea

Cause	Age	Appears Ill?	Fever	Stool appearance		Treatment
				Gross	Microscopic	
Excess carbohydrate in feed	Infancy	No	No	Thin, frothy, yellow	Excess starch	Formula management
Excess fat in feed	Infancy	No	No	Soft, greasy, bulky, yellow	Excess fat granules	Formula management
Breastfeeding: 'physiological diarrhoea'	Infancy	No	No	Green, mucous, scanty	Non-specific	No treatment necessary
Starvation	All ages	Moderately	No	Rare, scanty, green-brown	Non-specific	Gradual oral feeding
'Parenteral diarrhoea'	Under 5 years	Moderately	Yes	Non-specific	No pus	Treat disease, usually respiratory. Liquid diet, then soft diet
Epidemic D & V (viral)	All ages	Mildly	Slight	Non-specific	No pus	Nothing by mouth, then liquid diet, then soft diet
Salmonellae	All ages	Moderately	Moderate	Non-specific, may have pus	Blood and pus	Specific antibiotics, parenteral fluids as necessary, liquid diet followed by soft diet
Shigellae	All ages	Severely	Moderate	May have blood	Blood and pus	

Staphylococcal enterocolitis	Under 5 years	Severely	High	Mucoid, watery, purulent	Pus	Hospital treatment
Amoebic dysentery	All ages	Mildly	Slight	May have blood	Blood and pus	
Epidemic diarrhoea of newborn	Newborn	Moderately to severely	Slight	Non-specific	No pus	Parenteral fluids, liquid diet, antibiotics
Appendicitis, Meckel's diverticulum	All ages	Moderately to severely	Slight	Non-specific	Non-specific	Surgical
Intussusception	4 months to 2 years	Severely	Slight	Bloody with mucus current jelly	Blood	Surgical
Food poisoning (usually staphylococcal, up to 6 hours after a meal)	All ages	Moderately to severely	Slight	Mucous, may have blood	Blood, some WBCs	Parenteral fluids if necessary and nothing by mouth; then liquid diet followed by soft diet
Allergic diarrhoea: Cow's milk	Infancy	No	None	Yellow, bulky, mucous	Eosinophils	Use formula free of cow's milk
Other allergies	All ages	No	None	Soft mucous, bulky	Eosinophils	Elimination diet
Coeliac syndrome	Usually 2 years	No	None	Foul, greasy, bulky, frothy	Fat ± excess	Hospital treatment
Chronic ulcerative colitis	All ages	Mildly to severely	None	Small, brown, mucous	Pus and blood	Hospital treatment

Table 5.3 Incubation and isolation periods of some infectious diseases

Disease	Incubation	Isolation of the infected person
Chickenpox (varicella)	7–21 days, (usually 14–15)	Until all vesicles are crusted, usually 7 days after rash appears. Communicable from 2 days before rash appears
Diphtheria	1–6 days, (usually 2–4)	Until 2 consecutive negative swabs obtained from nose; never less than 4 weeks
Enteric group	3–23 days	Until convalescence *and* 3 negative stools after cessation of treatment
German measles (rubella)	14–19 days, (usually 17–18)	Until rash disappears. Communicable from 7 days before rash appears to 5 days after
Infectious hepatitis	15–40 days	7 days minimum
Infective mononucleosis	2–8 weeks	Avoid contact with saliva (e.g. via cups, toothbrushes) for 3 months
Measles	7–14 days, (usually 10–11 to catarrhal stage)	Not less than 5 days from the day the rash appears
Mumps (epidemic parotitis)	14–28 days, (usually 17–18)	Not less than 14 days from onset or 7 days from subsidence of swelling. Communicable from 9 days before swelling onset to 7 days after
Poliomyelitis	5–12 days, (usually 7–14)	Minimum 3 weeks
Scarlet fever	2–5 days	During the 10-day penicillin treatment and until negative throat swabs on days 11–13
Whooping cough	7–14 days to catarrhal stage, then 7–14 days to paroxysmal stage	Until the cough and whoop have ceased for 14 days; or if whooping persists, at least 4 weeks from onset of cough

Table 5.4 Diseases and infestations that can be carried by household pets

Dogs

Rabies	Fleas
Scabies	Hydatid disease
Salmonella	Ringworm
Campylobacter	Leptospirosis
Toxocara canis	Giardia

Cats

Rabies	Fleas
Scabies	Ringworm
Salmonella	*Toxocara catis*
Giardia	Campylobacter

Caged birds (pigeons, budgerigars and parrots)
Psittacosis

Otitis media

Otitis media may occur at any age, with one-third of infants under 1 year of age suffering from an attack. Causative agents can be bacterial, viral or non-infectious.

A red, swollen tympanic membrane is diagnostic. Pain (sometimes intense), effusion behind an eardrum, retraction or darkening of the eardrum are also suggestive symptoms. Fever is not reliably related either to the illness or its severity.

Treatment is generally antibiotic therapy which may need to be repeated, especially in infants. Antihistamines, decongestants and nose and ear drops have no proven value in the treatment, although they may relieve specific symptoms. Effusions may persist for some months after treatment and may require surgical drainage.

Serous otitis media (Glue Ear)

This condition is characterized by a build up of fluid in the middle ear, due to a dysfunction of the Eustachian tube. It may be associated, for example, with enlarged tonsils, cleft palate or allergic rhinitis, and associated hearing loss can be between 30—50 decibels.

Serous otitis media will eventually resolve itself, but intervention may be necessary to prevent educational and/or behavioural problems developing.

Treatment may be a course of decongestants, antihistamines or antibacterial drugs (e.g. Septrin). In persistent cases, operative options include

- Myringotomy
- Grommets
- Adenoidectomy

Acquired Immunodeficiency Syndrome (AIDS)

The period between infection with Human Immunodeficiency Virus (HIV) and the onset of AIDS symptoms may range from 6 months to more than 7 years. As yet it is not known whether all HIV infections will ultimately develop into AIDS. HIV has been isolated from many body fluids but only blood, semen, vaginal fluids and breast milk have been implicated in transmission. The documented modes of transmission are sexual, parenteral and perinatal.

Increasing numbers of children with HIV infection are being reported worldwide, most of whom have become infected in the following ways:

- Through being born to seropositive mothers. The overall risk of infection in these babies is estimated between 25 and 50%
- Through exposure to contaminated blood or its products, or unsterile needles/syringes
- Through skin piercing procedures (as of the ear and nose) tattooing, scarification, circumcision, etc.
- Through sexual contact

Diagnosis is extremely difficult in paediatric AIDS as the maternal antibodies persist in the infant's circulation for several months, thus making antibody testing unreliable in infants. Antigen testing, HIV culture in blood or tissue as well as symptoms are better criteria. 75% of children infected with the virus will develop non-specific symptoms at a very early stage and the progress of the disease is usually more rapid than in adults.

Fear and ignorance of HIV and AIDS are having severe effects at the personal, family and social levels. Children who have contracted AIDS are often treated as social outcasts in schools.

Breastfeeding and AIDS
The risk of HIV transmission through breastfeeding is not yet defined, but appears to be small compared to *in utero* or intrapartum transmission. The World Health Organization (AIDS Series 3, 1988) states, 'The immunological, nutritional, psychosocial and child-spacing benefits of breastfeeding are well recognized . . . (and) should therefore continue to be promoted.' The Chief Medical Officer of Health in conjunction with the DoH Expert Advisory Group on Aids recommends that women at risk of HIV infection should not donate milk intended for other women's babies. Any woman wanting to donate must undergo an HIV antibody test, and a negative result received before the donor's milk is accepted.

Routine childhood immunization and HIV
The WHO (AIDS Series 3, 1988) recommends that children who are HIV-infected should receive immunization in accordance with the standard schedules (see p. 85) Non-immunized children with symptomatic AIDS should not receive BCG. They should, however, receive the other vaccines (Table 5.5).

Children with HIV and/or hepatitis B
Special precautions must be taken at all times if a baby or child is either HIV-positive or is a hepatitis B carrier. A high standard of hygiene must be maintained, and disposable gloves worn when changing nappies, or dealing with cuts or vomit. A bag containing disposable tissues, plastic gloves, sticking plasters and nappy bags to seal up anything soiled should be taken on trips away from home. Any clothes or towels which do have any blood,

Table 5.5 Recommendations on the use of EPI* antigens in HIV-infected individuals in countries where the EPI target diseases remain important causes of morbidity

	Vaccine	Asymptomatic	Clinical AIDS
Infants	BCG	Yes	No
	Diphtheria, tetanus, pertussis	Yes	Yes
	Oral poliovirus	Yes	Yes
	Inactivated poliovirus	Yes	Yes
	Measles	Yes	Yes
Women	Tetanus toxoid	Yes	Yes

* Expanded Programme on Immunization

vomit, diarrhoea, or, in the case of boys, semen, spilt on them should be sterilized before going in the washing machine.

Children carrying HIV may be more prone to gastric upsets and minor infections such as thrush.

5.3   Skin problems and infestations

Skin rashes in babies are very common as babies' skin is particularly sensitive. In many cases these rashes are harmless and quickly disappear and no further treatment, other than reassuring the parents, is needed. This is especially important as the baby's skin is also very permeable to many substances (including steroids) in ointments and creams. If these skin preparations are used too frequently and in too great quantities side effects may ensue.

Rashes in older children are often difficult to distinguish and as a result are frequently misdiagnosed. A mother may, for example, say that her child has had German measles three times — but in two of these cases the rash may have been due to some other virus.

When a rash does not respond to conventional treatment and is still causing distress, referral to a dermatologist should be considered.

Nappy rashes in infancy

Common causes of nappy rashes
- Napkin dermatitis
- Infantile seborrhoeic dermatitis
- Candidiasis
- Atopic dermatitis
- Miliaria
- Intertrigo
- Napkin psoriasis

Napkin dermatitis
This is usually caused by soiled nappies being left unchanged for long periods. Bacterial organisms in the stools interact with the urine to produce ammonia, which is alkaline and causes burns and ulceration. The rash is usually confined to the genitalia, lower abdomen and upper thighs, but the flexures are not normally involved. Treatment is by changing the nappies frequently, not using plastic pants, and careful rinsing of nappies, adding a teaspoonful of vinegar to the rinse. Zinc ointment BP or zinc and castor oil ointment BP can help. In severe cases a short course of steroid cream is helpful, as long as there is no associated candidiasis.

Infantile seborrhoeic dermatitis
This may involve trunk, axilla, neck, face, behind the ears, eyebrows and scalp (cradlecap), in addition to the genital and anal areas. Treatment is with a short course of steroid cream; severe cases can be treated with 1% ichthammol in zinc ointment applied over the steroid preparation. Cetremide shampoo will help seborrhoea of the scalp.

Candidiasis
This is most usually caused by *Candida albicans* and the oral cavities of up to 40% of normal children are colonized with the yeast. Babies are often colonized shortly after birth, either from

the mother or other hospital personnel. Predisposing factors to candidiasis are neoplasia, immunosuppressive drugs, long-term antibiotic therapy, corticosteroids and iron deficiency.

In infancy a secondary infection with *Candida albicans* in addition to napkin dermatitis is relatively common. The napkin area may become raw with a red glazed appearance. Nystatin cream is usually effective therapy although miconazole and clotrimazole creams are also useful.

Atopic dermatitis (eczema)

Atopic eczema is much the most common type of eczema seen in childhood but it is rarely seen in children aged less than 3 months. There is usually a family history of atopic disorders. The condition characteristically starts on the sides of the face and later involves neck, wrists, anterior aspects of the arms at the crease and behind the knees. It may also involve the nappy area. The lesions are very itchy. The lesions are not always due to an allergy and are not helped by skin testing. Treatment is as follows:

- Having a daily bath with *Ung emulsificans* (which should be dissolved in boiling water from a kettle first)
- Oral antihistamines to stop the itching (these are not addictive)
- Appropriate topical steroids
- Appropriate clothing: cotton next to the skin
- Heat is the single most aggravating factor and attempts should be made to ensure a reasonably cool environment (and avoid overdressing) at all times

It is now thought that in some cases atopic eczema can be avoided by exclusive breastfeeding for 4–6 months (see p. 87).

Miliaria (prickly heat)

This is caused by obstruction of the sweat pores, leading to sweat retention. It is usually due to overdressing a baby or to a too warm environment. Treatment consists of cooling the baby's environment and removing clothing. Simple dusting with powder is the only topical application necessary.

Intertrigo

This is a traumatic dermatitis caused by sweat and friction. It usually occurs in the groins of fat babies. Treatment is by frequent washing and use of a bland dusting powder. Intertrigo and seborrhoeic dermatitis may coexist.

Napkin psoriasis

Closely resembles true psoriasis, with sharply demarcated scaly dark red plaques in the nappy area and also involving trunk and scalp. Most cases clear up satisfactorily with a weak topical steroid or zinc ointment. A very small number go on to develop true psoriasis.

Other skin problems

Athlete's foot (tinea pedis)

This is part of the ringworm group of infections. Clinical signs are maceration and cracking between the toes associated with itching and sometimes pain. Pustules or blisters may appear on the sole of the foot in severe cases.

Diagnosis is usually from the clinical appearance, but the fungi can be cultured. Treatment is by topical therapy used twice daily with a powder or cream containing tolnaftate, miconazole, clotrimazole or haloprogin. Treatment needs to continue for 2–3 weeks, and the affected area should be kept clean, dry and well ventilated. Resistant cases can be treated with systemic griseofulvin (see below for side effects).

Ringworm

Ringworm infections are characterized by ring-like lesions on the body (tinea corperis), in the groin (tinea cruris), on the nail (tinea unguium), or on the scalp (tinea capitis). The latter is accompanied by hair loss. Transmission is usually human to human, although tinea corporis is spread by animals. Diagnosis is clinical or by microscopic analysis of scrapings. Treatment is generally topical with an imidazole preparation and should continue for 10 days after apparent cure to prevent re-occurrence. Scalp ringworm (tinea capitis) requires oral griseofulvin. Side effects of this drug include headaches, gastrointestinal upsets, and rashes.

Parasitic skin infestations

Scabies

Is caused by the mite *Sarcoptes scabies*. It develops equally well on clean and dirty skins and normal washing does not dislodge it.

Transmission is by close personal contact; clothing and bedding are not significant in transmission. Incubation is as long as 6 weeks and symptoms include severe itching, particularly at night when the skin is warm. A widespread erythematous rash may occur in the axilla, waist, inner thighs, buttocks and possibly the wrists and ankles. This rash does not coincide with the sites occupied by the majority of the burrows.

Diagnosis is by finding the burrows and the live parasite (a white speck about 0.5 mm long) but this may be difficult.

Treatment is a single application of benzyl benzoate to all areas below the neck to all members of the family simultaneously. Reinfection does occur but is less likely in a sensitized person — however, itching may last for many weeks after all parasites have been killed.

Head lice

Head lice (*Pediculosus capitis*) are also known as nits. They inhabit and feed off the scalp which they actually prefer to be clean. Eggs are laid at the base of hairs close to the scalp and if they are more than one centimetre away from it they are probably already dead.

The eggs appear as shiny grey oval specks on the hair which do not brush off, unlike dandruff.

Transmission only occurs during head-to-head contact, and therefore conditions for spread are most favourable within a family.

Optimal treatment is easily carried out by parents, the whole family being treated at the same time. Prioderm or Carylderm lotion (which is better than the shampoo) is applied and left overnight (although the smell is rather repugnant) and then washed off. It is essential that the scalp is thoroughly moistened and that the recommended time scale is followed.

Warts and verrucae

Warts are due to a virus, and can affect any part of the body, but when affecting the soles of the feet are known as verrucae. The virus is spread by infection of abraded or moist skin. All warts disappear sooner or later if left alone — 30% or more go within 6 months and 65% within 1 year. In very young children it is best to wait for the expected disappearance of the warts.

Numerous remedies are available without prescription. Probably the most effective treatment is 40% salicylic acid plaster. The emerging warty material may be removed with an emery board to relieve discomfort. Children with verrucae do not need to be excluded from swimming.

More sophisticated treatment consists of freezing the wart with liquid nitrogen and then curetting, which is done by a chiropodist.

Acne — see p. 164.

Worms

Threadworms (*Enterobiasus vermicularis*), also known as pinworms, are the most commonly found worms in children and adults. They are most common in the 5−9 age group. Infection may be asymptomatic, but where symptoms occur, they are characteristically perianal and perianeal itching which may result in restless nights.

Diagnosis is by threads seen in the stools or identifying the eggs by pressing adhesive tape against the perianal area first thing in the morning and examining microscopically.

Treatment should include the whole family and is with Piperazine. Attention should be given to scrubbing the fingers and hands before each meal and after visiting the toilet.

Other worms which are endemic in the UK and widespread elsewhere are roundworms (*Ascaris lumbricoides*), whip worms (*Trichuris trichiura*), *Toxocara canis* (dog round worms), *Toxocara catis* (cat round worms), *Trichinella spiralis*, *Strongyloides*, *Sterocalis* and *Cestodes* (tapeworms).

5.4   Medicines

Drugs which may affect the composition of breast milk

The following are drugs where deleterious effects have been reported. They are *not* safe for nursing and donating mothers.

Amantadine	Cortisone	Primidone
Antineoplastics	Diazepam	Radioactive agents
Anthraquinone	Ergotamine	Streptomycin
Atropine	Iodine	Sulphonamides
Bromides	Kanomycin	Tetracycline
Carbimazole	Lithium	Thiouracil
Cascara	Phenindione	
Chloramphenicol	Potassium iodide	

Drugs where some doubt remains as to safety

Barbiturates	Methyldopa	Propanolol
Erythromycin	Nitrofurantin	Reserpine
Indomethacin	Novobiocin	Thiazide products
Isoniazid	Phenylbutazone	Tolbutamide
Laxatives	Prednisolone	Trifluoperazine
Meprobamate	Prednisone	Warfarin

Over the counter prescribing for 1−6 year olds

Analgesics (for pain and lowering temperature)
- Calpol — Paracetamol 120 mg/5 ml suspension
- Medised — Paracetamol 120 mg/5 ml, promethazine 2.5 mg/5 ml

- Junior Disprol Susp — Paracetamol 120 mg/5 ml s/f*
- Panadol Elixir — Paracetamol 120 mg/5 ml
- Junior Panaleve — Paracetamol 120 mg/5 ml s/f
- Junior Paraclear tablets soluble
- Junior Panadol soluble tablets
- Junior Disprol soluble tablets

Antidiarrhoeal and rehydration
- KLN Mixture — Kaolin suspension
- Kaolin Mixture Paediatric
- Dioralyte sachets — Fluid electrolyte replacement (FER) (cherry/pineapple/plain)
- Glucolyte sachets FER
- Rehidrat sachets FER (lemon/lime/orange)

Laxatives
- Dioctyl Paediatric Syrup — Docusate sodium 12.5 mg/5 ml
- Infant Glycerine suppositories
- Lactulose solution
- Magnesium Sulphate Mixture

Antispasmodics and antiwind
- Infacol drops — activated dimethicone 40 mg/ml liquid
- Dentinox infant colic drops
- Gripe water
- Gaviscon infant sachets
- Asilone infant suspension
- Calcium carbonate mixture co paed

Cough and cold remedies
- Tixylix
- Tancolin
- Benylin paediatric expectorant
- Robitussin junior cough sedative s/f

* s/f = sugar free

- Pholcomed s/f
- Pholcomed expectorant s/f
- Benylin with codeine
- Lotussin
- Galpseud linctus s/f
- Expulin paed linctus s/f
- Expurhin linctus s/f
- Dimotane co paed liquid s/f
- Dimotapp elixir
- Actifed expectorant
- Actifed syrup
- Sudafed expectorant
- Sudafed elixir
- Simple linctus paed
- Phenergan linctus
- Phensedyl linctus
- Wrights vaporizer
- Pickles snuffle babe vapour rub
- Cupal baby chest rub
- Ephedrine 0.5% nasal drops
- Afrazine paediatric drops
- Karvol capsules
- Vicks mentholatum
- Otrivine paediatric drops
- Byronia

Travel sickness
- Kwells
- Joy Rides
- Sea Legs
- Sea Bands — bracelets worn on wrists

Teething
- Dentinox teething gel s/f
- Nelsons teething granules (Homeopathic)
- Bickiepegs biscuits

- Teejel
- Bonjela
- Anbesol liquid
- Medijel

Vitamins/fluoride
- Abidec multivitamin drops
- Minadex tonic
- Vitavel liquid
- Orovite syrup
- Dalivit drops
- Adexolin
- En-de-kay fluotabs
- Fluoride tablets

Cradlecap
- SCR Cradlecap
- Cradocap shampoo
- Dentinox infant cradlecap treatment shampoo
- Pragmatar

Nappy rash
- Vasogen
- Sudocrem
- Conotrane
- Siopel
- Thovaline
- Drapolene
- Morhulin
- Morsep nappy rash cream
- Metanium
- Kamillosan — Chamomile oil & extract
- Getavlex cream
- Daktarin cream
- Fullers earth cream
- Zinc and castor oil cream — or with lanolin

Emollients/dry skin conditions

- E 45 Cream
- Morhulin cod liver oil ointment
- Infacare baby bath/Infacare baby lotion
- Johnson's baby oil/Johnson's baby lotion
- Calendula ointment — Homeopathic
- Vaseline
- Aqueous cream
- Ungentum merck
- Balneum bath oil
- Alpha keri
- Oilatum emollient liquid or cream

Itching skin conditions/allergy/minor wounds

- Calamine lotion
- Lactocalamine
- Caladryl cream
- Eczederm cream
- Savlon baby cream
- Vallergan syrup
- Phenergan linctus
- Piriton syrup
- Homeopathic

Headlice/threadworm

- Prioderm lotion or Suleo M lotion or shampoo
- Suleo C lotion or Carylderm lotion
- Pripsen sachets
- Antepar liquid
- Lorexane shampoo

Homeopathy is now widely considered as an alternative form of treatment, and there are a variety of homeopathic remedies available from chemists.

Further reading and references

Insley J., Wood B. (1982) *A Paediatric Vade-Mecum*, Lloyd Luke, London

Mok J. (1988) HIV Infection in Children, J. R. Coll. Gen. Pract. **38**, 342−4

Polnay L. (1988) *Manual of Community Paediatrics*, Churchill Livingstone, Edinburgh

Rendle-Short J., Gray O.P., Dodge J.A. (1985) *A Synopsis of Children's Diseases*, Wright, Bristol

Semprini A.E. *et al*. (1987) HIV Infection and AIDS in Newborn Babies of Mothers Positive for HIV Antibody. *Br Med J* **294**, 610.

WHO (1988) *Guidelines for Nursing Management of People Infected with Human Immunodeficiency Virus (HIV)*, World Health Organization, Geneva

6 Developmental problems

6.1 Language development

Language testing is the least understood aspect of child development, perhaps because it is more complex than either vision or hearing, being dependent on so many other factors. These factors include intelligence, attention span, auditory discrimination, articulation and cultural factors which influence vocabulary and sentence structure, as well as pronunciation and intonation.

The processes involved in verbal communication (Fig. 6.1)
Normally comprehension develops ahead of a child's ability to talk. Comprehension may, however, be affected although it may be less apparent as a child can become totally reliant on gestural clues.

Difficulty in talking clearly and conveying one's meaning precisely can be a considerable handicap, and it is important that speech and language difficulties should be referred to speech therapists as soon as they are detected — preferably in the pre-school years. Children with speech problems may also have learning problems with reading and spelling. It will therefore

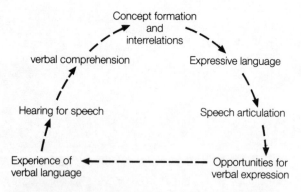

Fig. 6.1 The processes involved in verbal communication, from J.K. Reynell & N. Huntley, *Reynell Developmental Language Scales*, NFER, Nelson, 1985.

handicap the child least if appropriate treatment can be carried out prior to school entry.

Comparison with other children of similar age should not be made, particularly of siblings. Each child is an individual and should be treated accordingly.

An approximate guide to early language development

At birth normal range of cries including differentiation of pain and hunger cries

1 month makes noises other than crying. Coos in response to mother's talk from 5 to 6 weeks

6 months babbles tunefully to self; responds when spoken to; shouts when wants attention

8 months babbles repetitive strings of syllables, e.g. dada, mama, agaga, adaba

12 months knows own name; jargons conversationally and may have 2–3 clear words used appropriately, e.g. dada, mama

18 months begins to identify objects; combines two words as a complete sentence, e.g. Daddy gone, Mummy come

2 years forms simple sentences; has vocabulary of 50 words or more. Talks to self in monologues during play

3 years carries on simple conversation asking 'what', 'where', and 'why', questions. Loves stories, jingles, or nursery rhymes. Normal developmental non-fluency may be apparent at this age (see p. 154)

4 years conversational speech pattern should be developed; some double consonants may still be incomplete

Indications for referral
- If parents or carers are concerned
- If it is suspected that the child does not respond to sounds/speech
- No understandable speech by 2 years
- If the child babbles and then stops making sounds
- Any history from birth of feeding problems, e.g. sucking or chewing
- Unintelligible speech or limited to occasional words at 3 years; or speech consisting mainly of vowels
- Child repeating phrases which echo mother and have no meaning to him/her at 3½
- The child spoke early but shows frequent stammering at 4

Common problems

Failure to develop expressive language in the first place
This may be owing to:
- Lack of stimulation
- Audiological problems
- Emotional or psychological problems
- Low general intelligence
- Problems in motor development
- Specific language problems

Normal non-fluency around 3 years of age
This may be mistaken for early stammering, but is a stage of language development which children often go through. Attention should not be drawn to it and it should disappear spontaneously. If in doubt or the condition persists, then referral to speech therapy is appropriate as occasionally a stammer may develop.

Phonological problems at school age
The most common phonological problems are:
- S defects
- K pronounced as T

- G pronounced as D
- R pronounced as W

Many of these phonological problems do not cure themselves and may become a reason for children being teased at school. It is therefore better that problems receive expert speech therapy assessment in the pre-school year.

All children with language problems should have a full audio-metric test before further investigation, if appropriate

Language testing

There are a wide variety of tests available for speech and language development which should only be administered by speech therapists.

A quick screen of children's speech and language after the age of 3½ is to talk to and listen to the child; get him/her to talk about his/her toys, describe picture books or recite jingles and nursery rhymes. If she/he does not respond appropriately or there is any difficulty in understanding him/her, then referral for speech therapy assessment is appropriate.

6.2 Behaviour problems

Most behaviour in children only becomes a problem in relation to the parents' ability to cope with it. For example, it may have been acceptable for a child to sleep in the parents' bed, but the arrival of a new baby may cause this to become a problem.

Most problems can be dealt with by providing a sympathetic ear and simple common sense advice and support. The difficult decisions are when the problem overlies some actual pathology (for example enuresis caused by a urinary tract infection) and when the problem is so severe that it needs further help from a child psychiatrist, paediatrician, or clinical psychologist.

Breath holding and temper tantrums

These both occur in children usually under the age of 4, and almost always in a situation where the child is frustrated by something or someone. Neither is harmful to the child, although in a breath-holding attack the child may become cyanotic, which is often disturbing to the parents. Parents should be advised that they should try to keep calm during the attacks, not to slap or physically punish the child, but also not to give in if the attack has occurred because the child has been told it can't have something or do something. By giving in the parents encourage the behaviour. As far as possible frustrating situations should be avoided, but when the attacks do occur the child should be told quietly why he/she cannot do what he/she wants to do and then ignored, or his/her attention diverted to something else.

Head banging

This often occurs under similar situations as breath holding and temper tantrums and if this is the case the same procedure should be followed. However, if the child is banging his/her head hard enough to hurt himself/herself, then professional help should be sought.

In some cases children habitually rock or bang their heads through lack of stimulation or boredom. These are also patterns of behaviour more commonly seen in mentally retarded and autistic children, and in such circumstances different criteria apply.

Phobias

Phobias are irrational fears of such things as the dark, robbers or going to school. These are usually caused by factors other than the stated fears: for example fear of the dark may in fact be a fear that the parents may leave the house whilst the child is asleep. In most cases calm discussion with the child and the parents will give some clue to the cause, but if the fear begins to interfere with the child's normal behaviour, further advice from a child psychiatrist should be sought.

Masturbation

Parents should be reassured that this is universal, and the child doing it should be ignored and not punished.

Aggression

A certain amount of aggressive behaviour is normal from birth onwards, but needs to be harnessed and controlled. An infant who attacks by biting or hitting is best dealt with by loving firmness from the parent rather than return of aggression. Later, aggressive behaviour may be shown towards a younger sibling, usually as jealous competition for parental affection. Again this can be dealt with by loving but firm control from the parent and by channelling it into constructive behaviour such as helping the aggressive child look after the new baby.

Hyperactivity

This is extremely difficult to diagnose as a pathological condition. Most children are more active on occasions than either their parents or teachers can manage. However there does appear to be a very severe form of hyperactivity where the child is noted to be markedly overactive both at home and at school, with a very short attention span even when playing with new toys or watching television. In some cases this may be associated with adverse circumstances in the perinatal period, such as asphyxia. In these severe cases the child should be referred to a paediatrician, but in most other cases advice and reassurance is all that is needed.

6.3 Sleep problems

Night waking and bed refusal

Most children and adults wake up occasionally during the night, but the child who will not settle or who persistently wakes at night is a distressing and exhausting problem for parents. There may be a variety of contributory factors but the cause may be irrelevant. Practical help and advice is needed to solve the problem.

The pattern of established sleep problems, either in settling or night waking, with persistent demands for attention, will continue until the parents become desperate or resolve their ambivalence about setting firm limits. The technique in solving the problem is based on modifying the parents' response in order to alter the child's behaviour, and thus not give rewards.

A suitable bedtime, and a calming routine of preparation for bed, such as a bath and story, will help a child to feel safe and relaxed before being left.

The child who gets out of bed after he/she has been settled needs to be firmly taken back to his/her bed. This should be before he/she has managed to reach the comfort of the living room. The reasons for not wanting him/her to get out of bed should be explained and delaying tactics avoided. This process should be repeated until the child realizes that there is nothing to be achieved by this behaviour.

The child who continually wakens in the night needs to be settled firmly back into his/her bed, with the minimum of sympathy or contact, and for the parent to leave the room. If the crying continues, then after 5 minutes the same procedure should be repeated each time the child cries. After three or four nights the child will have learnt that crying no longer achieves the desired end.

Nightmares

These are most common around 3—4 years and are characteristic in that the child calls out, is fully awake, and can remember the unpleasant experience, although younger children may have difficulty in explaining it.

Usually comforting is all that is required, although certain factors, such as excitement or certain television programmes may be the trigger. Occasionally night lights or special toys may be needed for extra reassurance.

Night terrors

These are distinguishable from nightmares because the child is not awake, is difficult to waken and does not remember it either at the time or the next day. They tend to occur in older children and usually happen in the first few hours of sleep, at about the same time each night. They are quite terrifying for the parents, but can be avoided by wakening the child about 20 minutes before the expected time of the night terror.

6.4 Eneuresis and encopresis

Bed wetting
By the age of 3½ years 75% of children are dry and by 5 years 90%. Up to this age it is unwise to embark on any energetic form of treatment. The aim with the parents should be to prevent too much anxiety or stress being generated in the home, which in itself may interfere with the child becoming dry. After that age consultation with a doctor should be sought and investigations should include urinalysis for glucose, albumin, microscopy and culture. The problem should be discussed with the parents and child separately, and a confident and reassuring assessment of the outcome given, since the placebo response to therapeutic regimes for eneuresis is considerable.

Therapeutic regimes include:
• Eneuresis alarms are the most effective treatment for older children, generally not before 7 or 8 years
• Bladder and 'holding on exercises'. These help children to feel in charge of becoming dry as well as strengthening the bladder muscles
• Drugs such as imipramine and amitriptyline have limited useful-ness and do not have a lasting effect. They may have a usefulness in the short term, for example a child going on a school trip

Soiling or encopresis
Most children, particularly during the time they are becoming clean, have the odd 'accident'. These should be ignored. In a population of 7 year olds, soiling occurs more than once a month in 2.4% of boys and 0.7% of girls. Persistent soiling in an older child is a serious problem (see Fig. 6.2). The most common cause is constipation with overflow diarrhoea, and in these cases the constipation needs to be treated vigorously. Soiling can

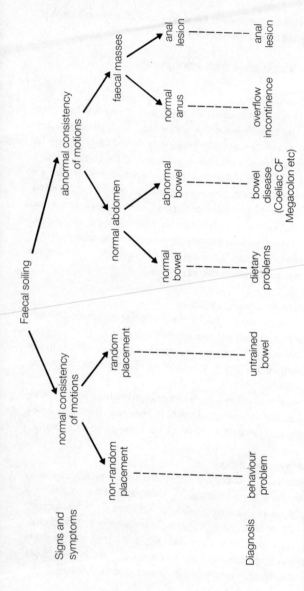

Fig. 6.2 Encopresis.

produce behaviour problems because of embarrassment, but it is rarely caused by such problems. Punishment never helps. A child who persistently soils may need referral to a child psychiatrist after a paediatric assessment.

6.5 The School Medical Service

The Court Report (*Fit for the Future*, 1979) has stated that the primary objectives of the School Health Service in relation to the education of children are:

1 To promote the understanding and practice of child health and paediatrics in relation to the learning process

2 To provide a continuing service of health surveillance and medical protection throughout childhood and adolescence

3 To recognize and ensure the proper management of medical, surgical and neurodevelopment disorders, insofar as they may influence, directly or indirectly, the child's learning and social development, particularly in school, but also at home

4 To ensure that parents and teachers are aware of the presence of such disorders and of their significance for the child's education and care

5 To give advice and services to the LEA as required under the Education Act and the NHS Reorganization Act

School entry

More effective pre-school surveillance and more efficient methods of transferring information between pre-school and school health services, could preclude the need for school entry examinations of children. This could be achieved if the parents were to become the holders of the child health records (see p. 2).

At the present time all children should be assessed between 4½ and 5½ years, and subsequently as necessary. The purpose is to identify all children who have or might have special education and health needs, and who need to be observed during their school life.

For the majority, who have had adequate pre-school surveillance, the examination can be limited. It should include:

- Any parental and teacher concerns
- Review of pre-school records
- Physical examination, including auscultation of the heart, if there is a specific indication or if no records are available to confirm previous medical care
- Measure height and plot on centile chart
- Check vision using Snellen chart
- Check hearing using 'sweep' test
- Immunization status should be checked and school nurses should be able to complete routine immunizations without a doctor being present (see p. 79)

Further screening tests and routine assessments

- Hearing should be tested as necessary, especially for those with no record of previous hearing test and for those at risk of hearing loss
- Visual acuity should be tested at three-yearly intervals
- Height measurements should be made if there is concern about a child's growth, or if previous records are either unsatisfactory or incomplete
- Colour vision testing using Ishihara plates at age 11
- Questionnaires for parents and children to complete on transfer to secondary school, including anxieties of parent or child regarding health
- School nurse interviews (with parents, parents and child, or the child alone, e.g. in secondary schools) may be of some value, but need close evaluation

Routine physical examinations of all children are unnecessary as are selective examinations of children with special health needs, unless their value can be assessed. Routine head and foot checks are no longer appropriate, but may be conducted at the discretion of the school nurse, with advice and treatment as necessary.

There is a wide range of other services available for families and children with behavioural difficulties. These include:

- Family and child guidance

- Educational psychologists
- Educational social workers
- Child psychiatry service

The school nurse is also the ideal person to educate teachers to be able to cope with aspects of medical problems, such as epilepsy, asthma, diabetes, skin complaints and infestations.

Children with special needs

The 1981 Education Act has recommended that where possible children with special needs should be educated in ordinary schools, either in the mainstream part or in special units within the school. However, the 2% of children with more serious special needs are mainly in special schools, and these children should be known to the local district multidisciplinary handicap team, and will generally be under the care of a local consultant paediatrician.

The role of school doctor and nurse will be important in assessing, advising, supporting, monitoring and in some cases treating and managing school age children with special needs.

There should be close liaison at all levels between the school health service, the schools and individual teachers and parents. This is important when children change schools, to ensure prompt transfer of information concerning their special health needs.

6.6 Adolescence

Adolescence is a testing time for parents and teenagers alike. Parents may need reinforcement in their roles as limit-setters and counsellors, whilst their children are exposed to certain kinds of decisions and pressures, such as drug use, the expectation of early sexual relationships, and worry about academic expectations and employment on leaving school.

Substance abuse and dependence

There is much coverage in the media of the problems of adolescents with regard to alcohol, tobacco and drug abuse. A survey in 1985 of 14–16 year olds in Oxfordshire showed that whilst most of them (98%) recognized the hazards of smoking, 21% were in fact smoking themselves. Drinking was common in all of them with 95% having had an alcoholic drink at some time and with 30% drinking regularly every week. The incidence of glue sniffing was 5%, with 9% having tried other drugs (Macfarlane *et al.*, 1987).

Many young people experiment with substance abuse out of curiosity, or because their peers do so. For most young people it is a passing phase, but for some it can become a habit. It is important that primary health care workers concerned with adolescents — such as school nurses — should be aware of the signs and symptoms of substance abuse and thus be in a position to advise (see Table 6.1).

Eating disorders

Anorexia nervosa (self induced starvation) and bulimia (self induced vomiting and/or laxative abuse) are increasing alarmingly. These disorders are more common amongst middle class adolescent females with obsessional ideals about their weight. They are characterized by gradual and/or significant weight loss which may alternate with binge eating and dieting. Excessive exercise may also be a characteristic. Treatment is controversial and varied and includes medical, nutritional and psychiatric support.

Acne

Acne results from enlargement of the sebaceous glands and increase in sebum production due to raised androgen output. The sebum may liquify and be associated with secondary infection. The condition is extremely common in teenagers with a peak incidence in girls between 14 and 17 years and boys between 16 and 19.

Acne causes a great deal of distress to sufferers because of its effect on the appearance and it merits attention because of these emotional aspects as well as the scarring it may leave.

Diet does not seem to play a causative part, although various

Table 6.1 Specific signs and symptoms of drug abuse

Substance	Signs and symptoms
ETOH.ethyl	Central nervous system depression, school and family dysfunction.
Cocaine	Excitability, restlessness, confusion, delirium, hyperactive reflexes, rapid pulse, elevated blood pressure, dilated pupils, exophthalmos, nausea and vomiting; Cheynes-Stokes respirations and seizures precede death; epistaxis, rhinitis early signs.
Marijuana	School failure, relaxation of inhibitions, inattentiveness, frequent association with alcohol abuse in troubled adolescents.
Glue and hydrocarbons (lighter fuel, gasoline)	Resembles alcohol intoxication acutely: euphoria, ataxia, sensory disturbances; drowsiness, stupor and brief coma follow. Chronically; nausea, anorexia, inattention, somnolence. Excessive salivation and malodorous breath. Gasoline sniffing may be fatal; glue rarely causes serious permanent effects; perinasal reddening.
Heroin and narcotics	Acutely causes euphoria, somnolence, respiratory depression, stridor, bradycardia, urinary retention, increased oropharyngeal secretions, coma, or death. Miosis (pupillary constriction) occurs with all forms but in varying amounts. Treatment of acute overdosage is with naloxone (Narcan). Extended use causes many complications including hepatitis B, bacterial endocarditis, and malaria. Behavioural disturbances similar to those of alcohol (or other drug) addiction. Needle tracks on arm are helpful in diagnosis but not always present.

claims are made that acne may be improved by avoiding chocolate or other enjoyable foods. Climate appears to influence it, as there is often improvement during the summer, possibly because of the action of sunlight on the skin.

Treatment should include encouraging the sufferer to avoid squeezing the lesions. Cleansing should be with a bland soap or other cleansing agents and topical application with benzyl peroxide preparations, starting with milder creams and progressing to stronger ones if necessary. Systemic tetracycline or erythromycin may be necessary on a continuing or episodic basis in more severe cases. Severe cases should be referred to a dermatologist for assessment and possible treatment with high dose clindamycin, hormone therapy and Isotretinoin.

Sleep disturbances

Late nights and erratic lifestyles probably contribute to the daytime sleepiness and fatigue which are common complaints amongst adolescents. However, neuroendocrine pubertal changes have been implicated and depression, narcolepsy and sleep apnea/hypersomnia syndrome should also be kept in mind.

Periods

The majority of girls will not suffer as a result of their periods, but dysmenorrheoa can account for quite a lot of days off school. For most the symptoms are relieved by paracetamol and a hot water bottle, but a few will feel really ill and miserable through every period. For those girls medical intervention is important as schooling may be affected. Periods may take several years to settle into a regular cycle, and some girls will feel tense and depressed before their period is due. Trying to avoid emotional problems and arguments with family or friends can help to relieve the situation.

Headaches

This is a common symptom of all age groups, even very young children. Whilst some children with headaches may look unwell, with pale faces and dark rings under their eyes, or become quiet and inactive, others may appear perfectly well. It is important therefore to take a child's complaint of headache as genuine as it may interfere with education.

• Late nights, especially amongst adolescents, can cause headaches, and is simply resolved by earlier bedtimes

• Migraine is now a recognizable problem in childhood

• Emotional and stress headaches also occur in children with pain arising in the muscles of the scalp and neck. The cause may be clear, e.g. bullying, academic failure, rejection by peers or family problems. The teacher is the ideal person to detect these

• Eye strain is often cited as a cause of headache, although it is rarely a result of a deficiency of focusing causing tension pain around the eyes

Investigation and treatment

• A simple acute onset of headache without any obvious predisposing cause may be treated with paracetamol

• Where other symptoms such as fever, drowsiness, vomiting etc. are associated, then medical referral may be necessary

• Severe recurring headaches which interfere with a child's life require further investigation

Depression

Depression in children can be missed because of the variations in clinical presentation depending on the child's age and developmental stage. The depressions are usually shortlived and may occur in reaction to depression in a parent. It is manifested by a cluster of symptoms that occur over time, such as denial avoidance, overactivity, aggression, hoplessness, persistent sadness and failure at school. Isolated symptoms of short duration may simply result from developmental or situational stress.

Suicide

Suicide is a desperate attempt to end an intolerable situation. Suicidal children and adolescents have generally sustained more losses and life stresses and have responded with increasing

isolation and withdrawal. A history of previous attempts, alcohol-
ism, and depression in parents and siblings may be contributory
factors.

Following a suicide, the parents, siblings and peers must cope
with guilt, anger, and shame in addition to grief. Supportive
services and counselling should be available.

Further reading and references

British Adhesives and Sealants Association (1984) *Solvent Abuse*,
BASA, Stone, Staffs

British Paediatric Association (1987) *The School Health Services*, BPA,
London

Dobson P., Horseman S. (1988) *I'm the Boss of my Bladder*, ERIC, Bristol

Douglas J., Richman N. (1984) *My Child won't Sleep*, Penguin, London

Gross E., St. Denis M., Macfarlane A. (1985) *The Child Health Manual*,
Blackwell Scientific Publications Inc., Boston, Massachusetts

Johns C. (1985) Encopresis. *Am. J. Nurs*. Feb. 153–6

Macfarlane A., McPherson A., McPherson K., Ahmed L. (1987) Teenagers
and their Health. *Arch. Dis. Child*. **87:62**, 1125–9

Rutter M. (1980) *Changing Youth in a Changing Society*, Harvard University Press, Cambridge, Massachusetts

Wakefield M.A., *et al.* (1984) A treatment programme for faecal incon-
tinence, *Dev. Med. Child Neurol*. **26**, 613–16

7 Community issues

Health and well-being may be influenced by the nature of the community in which people live, work or socialize. This influence can have favourable or adverse effects. For example, a rural community may seem ideal for young families, with lack of pollution and plenty of fresh air, but the reality may include difficulties with transport and isolation. Conversely, urban communities have easier access to facilities, but high rise flats or dormitory estates can also lead to isolation through lack of social contact.

7.1 Cultural considerations

The most basic premise of the National Health Service is that it provides the same standard of care to all according to their needs. It is the job of health care professionals working with a population which has differing health care needs to identify those needs and adapt the delivery of health care accordingly. It is important that in so doing care is taken not to undermine the group's ways of doing things nor to impose views and values upon the group.

Ethnic groups

An ethnic group is any group of people who have certain cultural characteristics which provide them with a distinct identification, perceived both by themselves and others. These characteristics may be religion, language or lifestyle, and may equally be applied to White and Black communities. They may all suffer from society's attempts to suppress or dismiss the culture of minority-communities. The term 'ethnic minority' is largely used to describe people from Afro-Caribbean or Asian communities, but the largest ethnic minority in the UK is the Irish.

Illness

The incidence of illness amongst different racial groupings varies considerably. For example, phenylketonuria is largely a disease of White people, routinely screened for in the neonate, whereas sickle cell anaemia has a much higher incidence amongst Afro-Caribbean races, but is not always routinely screened. The concept of illness varies considerably as well. For example, apparently minor illnesses such as coughs, colds and fever are viewed as inconsequential by GPs, but for many groups may herald epidemics of potentially lethal proportions.

Diet

Diet evolves from availability of foods, depending on climate, geography and patterns of agriculture as well as social factors, religion, culture and lifestyle. Each diet contains a balance of essential nutrients in the country of origin. When people migrate, however, they take their diet with them, and this may become unsatisfactory owing to prohibitive cost or unavailability. Respect is necessary for religious impositions concerning diet, but how far individuals follow such restrictions depends on the strength of their own religious views (see p. 101).

Religion and cultural beliefs

Religious and cultural beliefs can make compliance with existing health care either difficult or impossible. Many women, from a variety of different cultural groups, prefer to be seen and examined by a female doctor, especially during pregnancy and for family planning.

Most people, regardless of their background, make use of various sources of help and advice. This can range from experienced advice from family members, for example mothers or older female relatives, to traditional or alternative forms of health care such as herbalism, homeopathy, and acupuncture.

Attitudes vary and in some communities, for example Asians and Travellers, men and women lead separate lives, with pregnancy and childbrith considered as entirely female matters. It would be inappropriate to discuss such matters with male members of the household.

Communication

Communication is an important part in the effective delivery of health care. Ethnic minorities are more likely to be concentrated in unskilled and semi-skilled jobs, and may have communication problems with health care professionals.

The ways in which health care advice or instructions are presented has a significant effect on how much individuals remember, and whether they act on the information received. Previous experience of racial prejudice and discrimination is likely to influence minority groups' expectations of health care.

Ways of improving communication

- Allow more time and give plenty of verbal and non-verbal reassurance
- Write down important points clearly and simply
- Simplify English used
- Check back on each point made before moving on

For people who do not speak English, or for whom English is a second language, health care professionals can improve the situation either by using a qualified interpreter, or learning the client's language.

7.2   Single parent families

A single parent family is defined as a household with children, where the organization and daily responsibility for maintenance of home and child care is solely dependent on one parent. The most common reason for single parent families is marital breakdown. Bereavement, breakdown of a relationship and unmarried women having children are other reasons.

Having only one parent does not necessarily jeopardize the emotional and material security of childhood, but many single parents are disadvantaged either from social exclusion or poverty. Just over three-quarters of all single parents live on state income support.

This definition excludes abouth half of one parent families, because it does not include those families with dependent children over 16 years, or those living in a household with other adults.

Although it does not specify the sex of the parent, the majority are women. The proportion headed by a father has remained at 1–2% since 1971. The number of lone-mother families has risen from 8% in 1971 to 16% in 1988. There are an estimated 1 million single parent families, caring for about 1.6 million children.

Single parent families are more likely to incur housing problems, with fewer being owner occupiers. Poor living conditions, such as shared accommodation, overcrowded conditions and a lack of basic amenities mean that these families are likely to move house more frequently.

Children in single parent families are known to be at greater risk of infant mortality, accidents, sudden infant death syndrome, etc., and it is important for health professionals to recognize the needs of single parent families.

7.3 Divorce

In the United Kingdom, one marriage in three ends in divorce; by the age of 16 one in five children will have experienced family break up. It is estimated that 2 years after divorce, one in two children will have lost contact with one parent. A recent study (Wallerstein, 1989) has shown that, of children interviewed 10 years after the family break up, 37% still professed to experiencing a pervading sadness.

Divorce is a psychological emergency for children, and a time of major stress. The parents are preoccupied with their conjugal struggles, and may be less available, supportive and sensitive to the needs of the children in coming to terms with the situation without suffering social or psychological maladjustment.

The effect on the children of the loss of parental contact or continuing conflict between divorced parents can manifest itself through signs of anxiety, anger, irritability, depression, bodily complaints and deterioration in academic achievement. The child becomes burdened with extra responsibility and may show diminished self discipline, which can lead to delinquency, promiscuity, or substance abuse.

Health professionals should limit their role to that of child advocate, while empathizing with both parents. Parents intending to divorce should be encouraged to discuss the issue with professionally trained conciliators, who act as mediators through the difficulties of parting, and help parents to plan together for the best future care of their children.

7.4 Stepfamilies

The concept of a stepfamily, or reconstituted family, is not new. However, stepfamilies are rapidly becoming society's new family unit because of the increasing divorce rate and not, as in Victorian times, because of death. Stepchildren appear to be a new but less visible 'at risk' group, and in some respects appear to be more disadvantaged than children in one parent families.

The increase in stepfamilies as a result of divorce rates is reflected in the fact that one in three marriages is a remarriage for at least one partner, and one in six involves remarriage for both partners. The common feature of a stepfamily is that it contains children, with one or both partners bringing children into the new family home either permanently or on a part-time basis, i.e. visiting.

There is an increase in the number of divorces occurring in second and subsequent marriages. Whereas the majority of marital breakdowns in first marriages are due to parental difficulties, most failures in stepfamilies are as a result of difficulties between stepparents and children.

Health care professionals need to be aware of the problems faced by stepfamilies and to be sympathetic to their needs and able to offer advice and support.

7.5 Homelessness

Homelessness is now a national problem of rural as well as urban areas. It results from a lack of affordable housing and is precipitated by overcrowding, family disharmony and violence, previous sub-standard accommodation, loss of tied accommodation and eviction. The number of people losing mortgaged homes is rising rapidly.

Local Authorities are responsible under the Housing Act 1985 (England and Wales) to house anyone in the following categories:

1 if members of the household have no accommodation which they can legally occupy in England, Wales or Scotland; if they cannot return to their accommodation because they face violence or the threat of violence from someone living there; if their accommodation is a moveable structure, vehicle or vessel and there is nowhere they are able to place or reside in it; or if they are threatened with homelessness within 28 days.

2 if the household is a priority group, i.e. it includes:
- dependent children
- pregnant women
- those vulnerable through old age, mental illness or handicap, physical disability or other special reason
- those homeless or threatened with homelessness because of an emergency such as fire, flood or other disaster.

3 if the members of the household are not responsible for their own homelessness.

The local authority has to establish qualification for local re-housing on the grounds of previous residence, employment or family associations. If the homeless person does not qualify, the local authority may discharge its responsibilites by referring applicants to another area on grounds of local connection there.

Because of the substantial decrease in available public housing increasing numbers of people are placed in 'bed and breakfast' accommodation. Stays may vary from a minimum of 3 months upwards, with periods in excess of 3 years being recorded.

Health and homeless families

Homelessness causes an increase in mental illness, depression and postnatal depression. The stress and anxiety this causes can lead to a deterioration in family relationships.

Children suffer from overcrowded and often insanitary conditions. Infectious diseases spread more easily, diarrhoea and vomiting are common from poor water supplies and shared toilets. Upper respiratory tract infections are rife because of damp and the need to vacate premises by day. Infestations such as fleas, scabies, lice, bedbugs and mice are common.

Children in homeless family accommodation suffer emotionally and show a high incidence of behavioural problems, such as depression, disturbed sleep, overactivity, bedwetting, soiling, temper tantrums and aggression. Because of overcrowded conditions and lack of play space, their motor skills and speech development suffer. Older children have problems in doing homework.

There is a high incidence of accidents from unprotected fires, kettles and gas rings. Lack of safety features such as stair gates and poorly lit stairs, and lack of safe play areas for toddlers encourages falls. Accidents are common if a mother is under stress or depressed. Homeless children are more likely to be admitted to hospital and many children living in hotels are on the social services 'at risk' register.

There is evidence of malnourishment in both adults and children. Weight loss occurs in adults and there is a higher incidence of low-birth-weight babies. Women are twice as likely to have problems during pregnancy, and are more likely to be admitted to hospital during their pregnancy.

Temporary re-housing should ideally be within the family's own locality. GPs and health visitors should have a major role in ensuring that the homeless have access to proper health care, by adapting the primary health care services to the specific needs of the homeless. However, until legislation improves the lot of the homeless family, the future is bleak.

7.6 Debt

Rising unemployment with associated poverty, as well as easily available credit and escalating interest and inflation rates, have all contributed to a large increase in debt, and in particular multiple debt.

Families living on fixed incomes have found budgeting increasingly more difficult as essentials such as rent, fuel bills and food prices have continued to rise.

Mounting debts can lead to disconnection of essential services such as gas and electricity, repossession of home or hire purchase items, court action and even prison.

Before debts start mounting up, families should be advised to seek detailed money advice, or debt counselling. Some areas have specialist Money Advice Centres, but the Citizens' Advice Bureaux or Consumer Advice Centres also have skilled advisers.

The Debt Procedure
- Prepare financial statement, including income, expenditure, budgeting, income maximization — benefits, and creditor list.
- Deal with urgent matters (e.g. fuel disconnection)
- Begin negotiations
- Make arrangements with priority creditors
- Make arrangements with non-priority creditors
- Review matters at regular intervals

7.7 Poverty

Lahiff (1981) describes poverty as a condition of want, of insufficiency, or of deficiency. 'Living on the breadline is not simply doing without things, it is also about experiencing poor health, isolation, stress, stigma and exclusion' (Lakhani *et al.*, 1989). The main groups living in poverty are the unemployed, low-paid, sick and disabled, and pensioners. Families with children face particular hardship, and within this group one parent families are particularly disadvantaged.

Income support is designed as the 'safety net of the social security system', to protect the poorest, but it can fail to make adequate provision. The means-tested benefits which are available to 'top up' income, are often not claimed by those who need them most.

Health professionals should be aware of the benefits available, and of the advice centres in their areas where help and information can be obtained.

7.8 Benefits

A checklist of benefits which may be available

For the unemployed
- Unemployment benefit
- Income support
- Sickness benefit
- Invalidity benefit
- Housing benefit
- Community charge rebate
- Social fund payments
- Health and education benefits

For those in work
- Family credit
- Income support
- Disability employment credit
- Housing benefit
- Community charge rebate
- Health benefits

For single parents
- One parent benefit
- Income support
- Family credit
- Free milk and vitamins
- Health and education benefits
- Housing benefit

For the sick/incapable of work
- Statutory sick pay
- Sickness and invalidity benefit
- Disability benefits
- Income support
- Health and education benefits

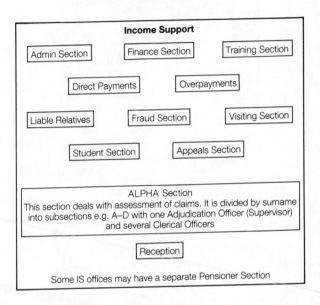

National Insurance benefits

(usually with Pension, Sickness and Invalidity Benefit, Child Benefit, SDA/Industrial Injuries Benefits sections)

Income Support

Admin Section   Finance Section   Training Section

Direct Payments   Overpayments

Liable Relatives   Fraud Section   Visiting Section

Student Section   Appeals Section

ALPHA Section
This section deals with assessment of claims. It is divided by surname into subsections e.g. A–D with one Adjudication Officer (Supervisor) and several Clerical Officers

Reception

Some IS offices may have a separate Pensioner Section

Social Fund

Fig. 7.1 The structure of a local DSS office.

• Housing benefit

The structure of a local Department of Social Security office is shown in Figure 7.1.

7.9 Non-means tested benefits

The top three boxes in Figure 7.2 contain the non-means tested benefits. Eligibility for these benefits is dependent either on National Insurance contribution record (top box), or paid as of

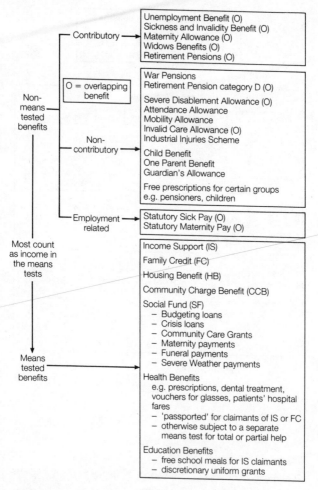

Fig. 7.2 The social security system.

right where some general condition is met — mainly disability, (middle box) or for those in employment (bottom box). In addition, all the benefits have specific and detailed conditions of entitlement which have to be met.

There are rules about overlapping benefits which prevent the payment of more than one of two similar benefits (marked 'O'). These benefits count as income when determining entitlement to the means tested benefits below.

Three important exceptions to this general rule are attendance allowance (AA), mobility allowance (MA) and disability allowance (DA), from 1992. These are payable on top of any means tested benefit without affecting that benefit.

Child benefit

Child benefit has to be claimed — there is no longer an automatic invitation to claim.

Eligibility for these benefits should be checked first, since if conditions are met, they are payable without any reference to a person's income or savings and are therefore reasonably straightforward to claim.

All these benefits can be 'topped up' by the means tested benefits in section 7.10, and in many cases this will be necessary.

7.10 Means tested benefits

The means tested benefits are in the bottom box of Figure 7.2. The following is a brief outline of these benefits. See section 7.13 for detailed information.

Income support (IS)

This is a weekly benefit paid to those with no other source of income or working less than 24 hours a week, *and* on a low income. It is typically paid to the unemployed, single parents and those sick and disabled who either do not qualify for non-means tested benefits or who have a reduced earning capacity. Unemployed people have to 'sign on' as a condition of receipt of IS, although there are exceptions to this rule, for example single parents and those incapable of work through sickness.

Young people (16 and 17 year olds) will only receive IS in special circumstances.

The means test has two elements: income (including other benefits, earnings, maintenance) and capital (including savings and available assets). There is a 'capital cut-off' where claimants with capital in excess of a certain amount are not eligible to claim IS.

Family credit (FC)

This is a weekly benefit paid to those in full time work (i.e. 24 hours or more a week), on low earnings and with dependent child(ren). Both couples and single parents are eligible, and once awarded, the benefit is paid for 26 weeks irrespective of changes in claimants' circumstances.

The means test is the same as that for IS.

Housing benefit (HB)

This is a weekly benefit comprising a rent rebate/allowance and a community charge rebate. For those in receipt of IS (or whose income is at IS level) maximum HB is payable. This is 100% of eligible rent and 80% of community charge. Service charges, meals, heating, etc., cannot be included in the calculation of rent for rebate purposes.

The means test has two elements: income (see IS) and capital. The capital cut-off is different from IS and FC.

Community charge (poll tax)

The community charge replaced rates from April 1990. It is payable by all adults who are solely or mainly resident in an area. Payment may be in instalments over a period of weeks or months (depending on the local authority). Couples are 'jointly or severally liable', which means that non-payment by one partner could result in enforcement action for payment taken against the other partner. Failure to pay may result in court action and imprisonment.

Those who are exempt

1 Prisoners and detainees — including both convicted prisoners and prisoners on remand, except those imprisoned for non-payment of poll tax or non-payment of fines

2 Visiting forces and specified international organizations

3 Severely mentally impaired people

4 18 year olds still at school for whom Child Benefit is still being paid, or for 19 year olds who are in further education. Full time students in higher education are liable for 20% of the poll tax

5 Monks and nuns who have no income

6 Long stay hospital patients and people in residential homes, nursing homes and hostels, where that place is their sole or main residence

7 Care workers employed for at least 24 hours per week and paid less than £25 a week and resident on the premises

8 Persons of no fixed abode

Community charge benefit

For couples, assessment is based on their combined poll tax bill and combined income. Maximum benefit is 80%, but everybody is liable for the first 20% without rebate.

There are no non-dependant deductions for community charge benefit as non-dependants, for example grown up children, grand-parents, lodgers, etc., will be liable for their own poll tax, and may qualify for rebate on grounds of their own income.

7.11 Social fund (SF)

This comprises a system of five different types of payments and loans payable in the main to those in receipt of means tested benefits or who have no other source of income in an emergency.

Maternity payment

Maternity payment is a single payment from the SF made to pregnant women if either they or their partner is in receipt of IS or FC.

Funeral payments

Funeral payments are available to those on IS, FC or HB, depending on savings, insurance policies, etc.

Community care grants
Community care grants may be available to those on IS to help
them lead independent lives in the community.

Budget loans
Budget loans are interest-free and repayable, and may be available to those on IS, who need help for an exceptional expense.

Crisis loans
Crisis loans are interest-free and repayable to anyone who is
unable to meet their needs in an emergency or following a
disaster.

7.12 Situations which may affect payment of benefits

Hospitalization
Payment of benefits is affected by admission to hospital. Attendance allowance stops after 4 weeks, although mobility allowance
goes on indefinitely for both adults and children. Personal allowances are reduced after 6 weeks, and after 52 weeks, entitlement
to housing costs is lost, and only a small personal allowance will
be paid.

   If a child is in hospital, then child benefit, one parent benefit and
guardian's allowance will stop after 12 weeks, unless regular
expenditure for the child is still incurred, for example by visiting,
buying presents, etc. *Disabled Child Premium continues to be
paid as long as the child is still treated as a member of the family.*

Going abroad
The UK has medical and social security agreements with some
countries. Medical rights should be checked before travelling.
Social security benefits may be affected by travel abroad, for
example, child benefit and one parent benefit cease after 8
weeks overseas. Further information is available from DSS
Overseas Branch, Newcastle upon Tyne NE98 1YX.

Benefits for immigrants

All non-contributory benefits are payable only if residency or 'presence' conditions over a certain period have been satisfied. All benefits, both contributory and non-contributory, are subject to the general rule of disqualification if persons are absent from the UK. However, there are many exceptions, and the DSS Overseas Branch (see above for address) will provide more information.

The European Community (EC)

Benefit while abroad within the EC may be payable either because the basic rules about going abroad apply, or under EC law. The general principle is free movement of labour within the EC. Legislation therefore applies to workers, former workers and their families. Further information is available from the DSS Overseas Branch (see above for address).

7.13 Advice and information — where to go for help

Advice Centres

These exist in most towns and cities in the UK. A full list is available from:

Federation of Independent Advice Centres, 13 Stockwell Road, London SW9 (Tel: 071 274 1839).

Citizens' Advice Bureaux (CABx)

These are available in most cities, towns and sometimes larger villages too. Staffed by volunteers, they offer a wide range of advice on financial, legal, consumer and general matters. Check local telephone directory for address.

Child Poverty Action Group (CPAG)

This is a national independent campaigning organization on poverty. They offer specialist knowledge on benefits, an advice line and assistance in individual cases. As well as publishing a variety of useful guides, bulletins, occasional papers, pamphlets and research reports, they also offer specialist training. Their address is:

Child Poverty Action Group (CPAG), 1 Bath Street, London EC1V 9PY (Tel: 071 253 3407).

Joint Council for the Welfare of Immigrants (JCWI)
This is an independent organization, not in receipt of government funding, which offers advice and assistance on immigration and nationality problems. Its address is:

Joint Council for the Welfare of Immigrants (JCWI), 115 Old Street, London EC1V 9JR (Tel: 071 251 8706).

Money Advice Centres
These exist in some areas — check in local telephone directory or CABs.

Law Centres
These exist in only major cities outside London. A list is available from:

Law Centres Federation, Duchess House, Warren Street, London W1 (Tel: 071 387 8570).

Shelter (National Campaign for the Homeless)
This is a national campaigning organization on housing issues. It offers specialist training and publishes the magazine ROOF. Its address is:

Shelter, 88 Old Street, London EC1V 9HU (Tel: 071 253 0202).

SHAC (London Housing Aid Centre)
This national organization publishes useful guides regarding housing problems. Its address is:

SHAC, 189A Old Brompton Road, London SW5 0AR (Tel: 071 373 7276).

Further reading and references

Barnes A. (1987) *Personal and Community Health*, Balliere Tindall, London

Caplan G. (1987) Guidance for Divorcing Parents, *Arch Dis Child* **62**, 752–3

Graham H. (1984) *Women, Health and the Family*, Wheatsheaf Books, Brighton

Graham H., Popay J. (1988) *Women and Poverty*, Thomas Coram Research Unit/University of Warwick

Hodder E. (1985) *The Step-Parents Handbook*, Sphere Books Ltd., London

HVA/GMC (1987) *Homeless Families and Their Health*

Lahiff M.E. (1981) Hard to help families, *Topics in Community Health*, HM & M, Aylesbury

Lakhani B., Read J., Wood P. (1989) *National Benefits Welfare Handbook*, CPAG, (1989) London

Macfarlane J.A. (1984) *Progress in Child Health, Vol. 1*, Churchill Livingstone, London

Mares P., Henley A., Baxter C. (1985) Health care in multi-racial Britain, *Nat Extn Coll*, Cambridge

Oppenheim C. (1988) *Poverty, the Facts*, CPAG, London

Robertson S. (1989) *Disability Rights Handbook*, The Disability Alliance ERA, London

Rowland M., Kennedy C., McMullen J. (1989) *Rights Guide to Non-Means Tested Benefits*, CPAG, London

Wallerstein J. (1989) *Second Chances*, Bantam Books, London

Index

Page references in *italics* refer to figures or tables.